Without a Voice
Angela Dukes
ISBN: 978-1-8382744-0-5

Published By: -

i2i Publishing. Manchester.
www.i2ipublishing.co.uk

Disclaimer

In order to protect others, some names have been changed, where appropriate. The writer had been away from Guyana since 1966 therefore some place names may have been changed. There is no intent to offend anyone. However, the writer apologises if anyone has been offended in any way.

Guyana is a land of many waters. A late 1960s change of name reflects its Amerindian heritage from its former name of British Guiana. The small South American colony on the top of the South American continent became a republic in May 1966 after being formerly divided into plantations owned and managed by slave owners from England, Holland, France and Spain. Following the emancipation of slavery, they returned wealthy to their homelands and earned titles. Guyana is bordered to the south by Brazil, east by Dutch Guiana or Surinam and to the west by Venezuela. Indentured servants from the Far East were brought in to continue the work of freed slaves which was to cultivate sugar cane, rice and copra, a constituent of the coconut processed to make coconut oil and other by products.

Guyana has a temperate climate throughout the year. Its rainy season is a complete deluge and reminders of non-school days because of severe flooding allowed children the opportunity to improvise boats, rafts or anything that would float. It was fun and wet, mostly muddy fun. There are many wet areas reflected in Guyana's lush vegetation and eventually endless supplies of seasonal fruit for marauding monkeys, macaws, parrots, beautiful birds and more uninvited wildlife into populated areas. There are numerous streams, three main rivers, and pools, many of which are festered with mosquitoes, frogs, snakes and the odd alligator in search of food. There is also a wide variety of fauna and flora, animals and birds, whose habitation remain mainly hidden in its dense rain forests along with the native Amerindians who lived and hunted there.

The large inter-related family practised an archaic form of religion, a system which revolved around patriarchs and matriarchs to discipline family members and choose partners for children as they reached the age of puberty. They retained overall responsibility and status over business, property and most of all related social and community issues. It was a battlefield to negotiate for a young, naive woman. She had known nothing but poverty and ghetto living which had forced her mother to overturn her own upbringing to reflect her new environment after she became a wife.

Angela grew up in such an environment and family control over her life. The wider family were themselves divided through marriages; some left or changed their religious affiliation. Generally, though, the males had limited freedom to do as they desired, but the women were not allowed to make decisions for themselves or for younger females. This often led to boredom and gossip as a means of occupying themselves. From an early age girls were groomed to be servile to males even to their own brothers. To go against the accepted norms meant that physical or mental pressure would, on occasion, be exerted to correct any perceived rebellion against the cultural discipline. So, it was that in a large extended family, older males were regarded as elders. The duties of being an 'elder' continued until his death and then the next in line took on that responsibility. For the females it was similar, the older aunt or grandmother had the final word on any problems that the women experienced. If it was a problem which needed permission from a male elder, then the case would be passed upward via the eldest female only. Often, this would cause more anxiety since the problem might be embellished or downplayed. Thankfully, this practice has disappeared with the aid of younger folk; the rebellious as they were dubbed.

This was the how Angela existed from birth until she turned twenty. Her mother had related snippets of her own previous life in order to preserve some degree of dignity both for herself and for her two surviving children out of five. Her life was of reasonable affluence, a shared existence with her younger eight siblings and a father who ran his home with absolute authority. This included his wife whom Angela learned was a young beauty who had suffered great physical and mental cruelty from her husband until her early death. Apparently, though he was generous and considerate to employees, people of unfortunate circumstances whom he considered worthy of empathy. Not so to his own family.

Her father dabbled in politics, acquired properties – as was the cultural norm to provide each eventual married son as wedding gifts. For daughters, fathers gave dowries – as though they were for sale. He owned islands and businesses, he provided costs towards the erection of a church for his workforce and at least one outstanding community contribution – funds towards the provision of artesian wells for fresh drinking water. His nine children were expected to contribute towards the upkeep of all his businesses as well as the home, which included the management of a general merchant store attached to their family home.

Ash, Angela's grandfather, appeared to have been a self-made individual who believed that he was also above the law. Following the death of his young wife, he remarried a single parent with two grown up children. This marriage appeared not to have worked out for him, so he divorced her to wed another single woman. Angela did not know why her father died aged fifty-four. No foul play was suspected, it was simply accepted that folk died younger than was expected at that time. She was told that her grandmother had died at an early age too.

Following Ash's death, the wives disagreed about the division of his estates. From an account related by Babs, Angela's mother who was also the eldest of his nine children, it seemed that the second wife demanded her and her children's shares even if her marriage to Ash was fairly brief. The third wife kept out of the war and allowed Ash's sister (their aunt) to intervene and to settle the dispute. His youngest son was to be allowed only a nominal amount since he was under the age of consent which was twenty-one. This harsh treatment had caused him anger and, in his haste, and fury he had alerted the authorities about all properties and estates owned by the family. His action had devastating results for all the children. The entire estate was confiscated pending non-payment of taxes on a few of the properties.

All the children who were fortunately grown to the stage of young adults, were disinherited of any part of his estate. They became homeless, ordered to leave their home, forfeiting all, even the personal jewellery worn on that day when the authorities arrived. The youngest son forever after became ostracised from his siblings and would eventually be forced to emigrate. Angela's mum took on the responsibility to advise and to arrange for her brothers and sisters to either marry or to seek paid employment and that had left herself - closer to thirty-years-old, homeless and penniless. Her mother's brother, Uncle Walt and his family of eight, invited her to live with them.

Her former home with its attached general store was situated on the other end of Peter Rose Street from Uncle Walt's home which was a large, impressive and imposing white painted two-storey house with a large veranda at its front corner. The property was in a residential location and stood on the corner of two streets, Crown Street, the main highway and Peter Rose Street which led into the residential part of Queenstown possibly named in honour of Queen Victoria many years before. It sported a beautiful rose garden and the perfume from the jasmine tree when the flowers were in bloom was savoured by passers-by for its heady scent. Beyond the rose garden grew a huge old local grape tree which in season had an abundance of lush, sweet purple grapes. Babs's Aunt Imelda made her famous grape wine each year if she was able to collect enough fruit before her own and other local children helped themselves to feast and to take home.

On the opposite side of the home on Crown Street was a sports ground with its own pavilion funded and built by the families and affluent locals for community events. The family was certainly large and extended therefore there was no shortage of participants for gatherings or events, and friends, acquaintances and neighbours were privileged to be invited to events.

It was in these surroundings which had so greatly impressed Angela's own father Joseph who had assumed that there was the probability of a large dowry if he was able to convince those folk that he was genuinely interested in one of the girls. It was on a day when the family played cricket – a team that was made up of ten family males and one friend. Joseph stopped on his bicycle to watch the match but spied an opportunity when his eyes homed in on Babs who was among the women as they watched the match from the veranda.

He had then taken the opportunity to enquire more about her, from her male cousins and they told him what he wanted to know. A couple of them thought it was an opportunity for her to be eliminated from any possible inheritance from their father so they perceived him to be a potential suitor. Babs tried her best to be grateful to this family but a couple of them regarded her as a burden and used her gratitude for their own purposes. They pressured her to accept the man's proposal. She had eventually succumbed, tired of their persistent remarks and jibes. She was given in marriage by her uncle, but never spoke to Uncle Walt not being aware of her discomfort within his family.

After that initial sighting and gathering of details he had sought out the company of that same cousin to apply pressure for him to be introduced as a suitor. Her Uncle Walt had no idea that she was unhappy nor would she ever complain. He had been very generous to take her in and to include her into his own family of six children. Therefore, he was delighted to see her settled if she wanted to.

After the wedding, her mother never talked about it or any celebration itself. Angela, as a primary school pupil, had recalled a photograph of the wedded couple hung on a wall of another relative's house but it had disappeared. Her father had expected to receive a dowry because that was the only reason that he had actually wanted to marry Babs. She lived in that impressive house so surely there would be a healthy dowry, as it was customary for wives to come with dowries.

However, Joseph's wedded bliss became snowflakes and melted just as quickly. Unfortunately, the marriage did not last for long either when he learned that there would be no dowry. His eagerness to have Babs as his wife dissipated. He rented a one-room slum dwelling for them to call home. He began to mentally abuse her; she must ask her rich family for money because he did not have enough for them to live on. When she refused, he physically abused her. Joseph was a peddler who sold fabric from rolls of materials carried in a butcher's tray on his bicycle, to folk mainly in the countryside who were themselves just as poor, so bought lengths of fabric on tic – in lieu of payment on the last day of each week.

Back in the slum ghetto which became Babs's home, the rent collector also called each Friday to collect from the tenement dwellers. At the same time Joseph had collected his earnings from the sale of materials and returned to spend almost all of it in the local inn. Some paid but not everyone was able to since poverty was rife in those areas also. As a toddler Angela remembered one early Saturday morning when he had finally meandered his way home drunk and singing loudly the only song he knew the lyrics of *Waltzing Matilda* and arrived home swinging a dead chicken by its legs and the newspaper-wrapped gift for Babs - a dead fish. Apparently, these were given to him in return for his generosity to treat all to drinks until his funds ran out or his friends were unable to swig more rum.

Meanwhile, Babs hid from the rent collector waiting for Joseph to return with money for the rent and to buy milk for the baby. Angela was three when her sister arrived to become another member of the hungry, neglected family. Her mother often needed to open the door before Joseph had the opportunity to cause a disturbance by shouting or banging on the door. He fell in rather than stepped in then headed for their only chair to drop into it or miss and slip to the floor still holding on to his goods. It took him a while to assess his surroundings before the chicken and gift-wrapped fish was handed over. This was very inconvenient for Babs because she had to set about preparing both and then to cook them in the makeshift kitchenette outside, before they went bad. They were also food for the hungry family which had to last for a few days at least.

First priority was to ask for money for the rent, then if any was left, she needed to buy milk for the baby. This was his cue to loudly berate her for badgering him constantly for money. Why did she not go and ask her rich relations for the money? He was obviously devoid of any responsibility for his household. The walls were constructed of thin wooden planks and his voice carried beyond their own room to eager ears to be related later to others.

There was no partition between their bedroom and living room and so Angela watched her father's antics with amusement. Her giggling was stopped when her mother told her to go to sleep, which was very hard to do in such an environment, The charade went on for a while until he fell asleep where he sat or fell or puked and Babs cleaned the mess. She got little sleep anyway, as the meats needed her immediate attention. As for any money she was fortunate to retrieve the few remaining coins from his pocket. There was seldom enough to pay the rent or to buy milk and food for them. So, she juggled whatever money was forthcoming and continued to hide with embarrassment in order to feed her two young children.

Angela herself had known no other existence apart from living in ghettos where she was not allowed out to play because she would be bullied, and her meagre collection of toys stolen. To protest or complain would cause her Mum, to suffer retribution from other women. Her early years were spent confined to their one room downstairs dwelling that served as bedroom and living room. Even the only window at the back of the house was unsafe to open for air because tenants above so hated Babs that they emptied their waste over that window. The cooking facilities were separate. Upright shacks situated in front of the building of each house consisted of a storage type of wooden hut with just one shelf to accommodate the iron coal-pot used for cooking on and an adjoining shelf/worktop. No food or valuable stuff such as utensils or ingredients remained overnight as these would be stolen. The place was overrun by rats which emerged during the evening from the alley at the back of the slum. They were large, daring and competed with the dogs for food scraps.

Her Mum did her best to cope with the circumstances she had found herself in, but it was an unsafe environment even for her – because of Angela's father. He was an ambitious individual who wanted instant wealth and the trappings that came with it. Also, he was besotted with his first child, Angela, who was his prized possession. Babs had lost two babies before Angela. Joseph occasionally remembered to bring a little treat for the young Angela and had given her a huge pretty doll. Then Angela received treats of glass marbles which she loved because of their rainbow colours and shiny smooth touch. Babs later related to her that Joseph took all the meagre savings which relatives had gifted to the baby Angela and kept them in a savings book for his own use.

Babs became tired of her situation: always, in danger of physical attacks, and the constant hunger of her children. The odd times when Joseph was at home, it was to sit with some of the men over cards and beer, get into a stupor and spill his domestic woes. He had acquired a small following of empathetic supporters of his cause, his wife was unreasonable and they shouted insults at her as she cooked or went by. Most did not need to walk past Babs's home but by doing so they were showing her that they could abuse her at any time. This ranged from verbal to physical abuse and she felt vulnerable for herself and for her children.

Acting on the advice of Aunt Tania (her mother's sister) and her cousin Olivia because Joseph had failed to provide security or food for his family. She decided to leave him and those horrible slum tenants. One Saturday morning before dawn, well before he appeared in his drunken stupor, she went into action.

Taking the small case which she had secretly prepared and hidden - a twelve by ten-inch tiny case packed with mainly baby things – and, carrying the baby in her left arm, she took the children and left praying to make a quick but silent exit. Barking guard dogs however ran after them, the dogs' owners emerged to shush the dogs but this loudly alerted others to Babs's leaving. A small group approached with loud jibes and taunts, but Babs ignored them and continued to head for the entrance. One eight-year-old girl had other ideas though. Egged on by her mother who would step up to physically intervene if Babs had stopped to defend her child, the girl approached the three-year-old Angela and delivered a resounding slap to her cheek. Babs understood the tactic and wisely she looked at Angela and told her to keep walking. It was to safety for them all Angela understood that and obeyed without a tear, and although her face stung, she never cried. It would not help.

She walked the couple of miles with her children from the city area to the edge of the suburb to her aunt's home. A tired and exhausted Angela was sleepy, but her mother constantly encouraged her saying just a little way more. The young Angela had learned to walk long distances. There was just one occasion that she recalled when her father took her out. He had settled her in the tray of his bicycle and had taken her somewhere to sit with him as he drank with other men. She remembered that incident because her Mum was not pleased when they eventually returned.

However, when the trio arrived at the aunt's home it was to receive a chiding. Why did Babs do such a thing? Where would she live without any money and with two small children? When the chiding ceased, she and the two children were temporarily bedded on rags beneath the dining table alongside their unpaid servant: Another relation who had learning difficulties and was easy to exploit. It was dawn anyway and Babs had no time to rest so she left the children in their care to seek somewhere for them to live and perhaps also employment of some sort.

She would later appeal to the elders of the family for a possible solution where she might be able to safely house and earn for herself and the children. As usual this same aunt was adept at re-interpreting the request to include her thoughts on any subject - as Angela learned over the years. It was a request for the family to grant her a loan, to rent or purchase a small shop. The loan would be repaid and the business would be as a home for her and her children. This request was refused three times. She was a woman and was advised to remarry so that some male would provide for them. Babs was refused on the grounds that money could not be loaned until she produced some form of collateral as this would be considered a business transaction.

She would go away unwilling to make such a commitment so soon after her freedom from an abusive and austere marriage. The elders however, continued to refuse her proposal and agreed to small handouts to tide her over. She needed to beg for everything from them as they applied more and more pressure to force her to accept their suggestion. She even needed to book appointments to speak directly to the elder and they made her wait hours. Angela remembers the anxious wait, the hunger and thirst for both herself and her Mum and the dismissal with a few coins from a bored elder.

One solution which was suggested by the family elder was that the three-year-old Angela should be adopted into his family thereby leaving Babs with the baby. Perhaps, it would be a better prospect for her to find a suitable husband. Babs would eventually and reluctantly agree to this, too worn down in her spirit to protest. Angela recalled the appearances of pretty cotton and organza frocks, the crocheted socks and shiny shoes she wore while she constantly asked, 'where were the frocks for her sister too'. Babs never replied but would hedge or divert those innocent childish questions.

Then they were summoned to visit this elder for a decision. Angela loved visiting that house. Well, not the house as such, but the entrance way that led to the wide front steps and porch overlooking an arbour of jasmine flowers. They were not scented as those in Uncle Walt's front garden but to Angela it looked like a bridal walk. When in bloom, the tiny white flowers dropped on to a path of smooth round pebbles from the gate to the wide front steps. Her one request for pretty frocks was that they should have pockets – to collect round pebbles, glass marbles, flower petals, feathers and any other pretty collectables. Her Mum would be left to launder away the stains.

Babs was told that she had no collateral and therefore would not be able to borrow any money. However, their joint solution was that the elder uncle with his similarly aged children would adopt Angela, then five. This would allow Babs the opportunity to look for a husband to look after her and the younger child. No man wanted the responsibility of Angela – she was considered too old.

The elder was in fact a prominent political figure, an esteemed businessman and a well-respected figure in the country. Many years later into her late teens and to Angela's chagrin he appeared as a director within the firm where she was employed. They had acknowledged each other briefly from a distance only, but from then on her boss paid special attention to her. Angela had been unaware of her myopic vision and constantly missed her lunchtime slot. One day, she was sent a message to visit the nearby opticians. This was a mystery because she had no funds to pay for tests or glasses, however both of these requirements were offered and paid by the firm. It was then that she realised it was the intervention of her uncle, the elder! No amount of evasive tactics to disassociate herself from her relations would ever go unnoticed. Even strangers referred to Angela as Ash's grand-daughter and not by her own name.

On their summons to his residence that day, Angela, then five, was ordered to enter a line up with his three children, seven, six and a three or four-year-old. The seven-year-old was a bully – like her papa – and unfortunately rubbed up Angela the wrong way. They resembled each other but also held a shared dislike for each other. The elder summoned cook to bring something for Babs and Angela to eat.   He assumed that they were hungry. So, the two sat to share the leftovers from the recent family meal which was plonked by a hostile cook, on to the large family dining table and they were ordered to eat. It was a piled platter of some rice dish and her Mum managed a small amount.   Angela struggled with her portion – cook deliberately piled a disproportionate amount before the toddler. Both received disgusted glances from cook or snide remarks from the elder such as "why don't you eat more? You said that you were hungry".

He surveyed the children in his military style line up and then turned abruptly to speak to Babs, to ask if she had made a decision about Angela's future with his family. That was the day that Angela learned why she had been pampered with pretty things for the past six months. She was groomed by him to fit into his family as collateral for a loan for her mother. She decided to leave the discussions to the two grown-ups and ventured on to the wide-open front balcony and inevitably down to do what she liked to do – collecting pretty bits beneath the jasmine arbour. It also allowed her distance between herself and the seven-year-old who was intent on bullying her. So Angela headed for her favourite place outside.

Before she could safely do so however, she had asked the eldest girl whether their two huge Alsatian guard dogs were locked up. Yes, they were locked up, the-seven year old replied so it was safe. As Angela ventured down to the third step there came an ominous growl, and she saw a flash of grey as the closest dog mounted the steps. She was forced to wedge herself between the newels to stare into the throat of that dog as he edged closer growling. At the sound of his growl, the elder came to the window and saw Angela. He shouted at the dog to go. The seven year old whined somewhere inside – 'Daddy I told her that the dogs were out, but she would not listen to me'.

It was a heart-stopping moment for Angela, but as soon as she was able to recover from her fright, she became angry and let him know how she felt about his proposal to adopt her. Until that day she was unaware of that plan but when he began shouting at her mother that the child's behaviour was that of a street urchin Angela let rip in reply. She did not want to be part of his horrible family and his wailing wife, who seemed to be forever ailing. Angela added that he was also a bully so was his daughter.

That person, his wife, was rarely seen but she would be frequently heard from the closed balcony above. It was common knowledge to all the family that his wife was unwell. Her days were spent reclining on a chaise lounge, and with her drama queen's voice she complained about "the noise" any noise which she said that gave her headaches. Angela remembered the one occasion when she had followed the children upstairs and she went past the reclined aunt, who stared at Angela and began to wail about too many children making noises. She then rang her little bell for cook to bring her a glass of something and perhaps a couple of pills to ease her nerves.

The young Angela thought the whole performance was pretty silly but remained silent. She never ordered the other children to go but complained to cook that that child – Angela - had caused her head to ache and cook should take the child away. Her husband must have discussed the probability of Angela joining her brood and she did not welcome the idea.

The street urchin and her hapless mother were ordered to leave by a dumbfounded stuffed shirt who had never been shouted at by a five-year-old. Angela though was happy to oblige.

Babs had little option but to continue to ask for assistance. This was refused many times. She was a woman and was advised to remarry so that someone would provide for them. The elders, however, continued to refuse her proposal and agreed to small handouts to tide her over. She needed to beg for everything from them, and they applied more and more pressure to force her to accept their suggestion. The pressure, ill-health through lack of proper food, her children's needs and constant begging, took effect and she caved in to do as she was advised - to re-marry. She was sent to a single man or a widower, to be interviewed as to her suitability for his requirements.

Angela accompanied her. It seemed that she was the deciding factor in most of her mother's dilemmas. To Angela, the man looked gross, ugly and sly. He sat across the small divide in his dirty upstairs flat. He smelled of fag ash, and appeared unwashed, as did his clothing. He sat open legged on a stool facing them, Babs was motioned to sit on the only unstable chair opposite while Angela stood beside her, and paid attention as he fired questions. Angela noted the baleful stare he directed at her as he questioned Babs. He wanted to know how many children Babs had before he would make his decision as to whether she would be suitable. Finally, he told her he would take her and the younger child. That one – a brief fag pointed at Angel – he told her; she must get rid of. Babs rose and with the words 'I will not throw away my children for anyone' they left that zoo-smelling flat.

Angela's memory of those bleak, uncertain days begun to blur with the number of moves into temporary accommodation, her somewhat sporadic education and hunger. They lived temporary existences in the oddest of places until they were suddenly ordered to go away into the countryside. Angela was confused. Why? Why were they not also allowed to take their meagre possessions? All that Babs owned was to be placed in the care of yet another relative who never returned them. That woman told Babs it was a waste of time since Babs and her children lived like gypsies. Her china dinner service was the only material possession she really loved and was what was left intact of a full dinner service – and a wedding gift.

It was not until she was a lot older that she understood why they needed to leave to live in the countryside. In the previous below the kitchen chicken-house which was a temporary place to call home, an incident had occurred. An uncle unexpectedly appeared and offered a reluctant Babs a few coins to purchase food for the children. He learned of her situation from gossip by other relatives and decided to use the dilemma for his own gain. She was desperate to feed her children and decided to overlook caution. He, apparently, had a reputation of being a lecher amongst other things. Anyway, he was her cousin so she accepted his coins. One evening, Babs blew the oil lamp out and settled down to sleep on the covered pallet she had improvised for a bed on the earthen floor. Angela then bedded down on the shelf which formerly held nest boxes, while her younger sister had a box for her bed. She was snug in there.

The door, held shut by a simple wooden latch, was opened and the six-foot man entered. Babs was fearful, she was aware that he could be violent. So, she pleaded with him to go. Those pleas were ignored, and the tearful Babs was violated. Angela pretended to be asleep but was concerned for her Mum witnessing how she sobbed and begged him to stop and to go. He repeated, 'Well, you owe me and it will soon be over.' The following days were a bit blurred for Angela, she felt sorry to see her mother in tears every day, and it made her feel helpless and confused. Babs duly reported his violation to that pretend-to-be-caring aunt who relayed her own version of the forced violation to the then head of the family, and as was the usual cultural response, she was blamed for encouraging him. The order to leave for the remote countryside was the solution given when Babs reported that she was pregnant. She had brought disgrace to the family and needed to disappear. Actually, she was verbally abused by the talebearer and consequently by the elder.

About ten miles into the countryside, she managed to secure an empty downstairs two-roomed furniture-free flat and a job that required a three-mile walk into the back-dam beyond the cane fields to housekeep each day for the plantation owner. She left each morning just past six after seeing to the children. The younger one was left in the care of the landlady, the older, who was Angela, would be at school until three thirty when she would return to care for her sibling, until Babs returned home at six thirty. There was nothing to eat for lunch, so Angela got used to going hungry. She had noted that her mother appeared to have gained weight, but she never commented about it.

That was the first proper schooling for Angela as she approached eight.   Up to then, her education had been hit and miss. Enrolment to "new" schools seldom went well. Angela was left to catch up or was simply ignored and would ask to be excused to sit in a quiet corner outside the building until the bell sounded to return to class or to go home. It was an ordeal for her, she was a late learner and needed to ask her Mum for help. Babs, though tired, always obliged as much as she was able to.

Eventually, one day she arrived home from school and was surprised to see her Mum there. They went to the local shop together which belonged to a relative or an acquaintance. They

27

were led into a back room. Hovering in the background were a couple of women who Angela –ignored. Perhaps she had assumed that they were merely curious, and it was a common reaction from people in that area anyway. Babs and her children were townsfolk and were regarded as curious.

On the floor lay a tiny new-born baby on a few rags. Her mother asked her what she thought of it. Angela recalled that childish discourse well. It went: 'It's okay.' 'Do you mind if he came to live with us?' 'No, but where will he sleep?' 'Oh, he'll sleep next to me, your sister will move closer to you.' 'Are you sure we can keep it; doesn't anyone want it'? These were important issues for Angela for two reasons - the three of them slept on rags on the floor, and her mother with her kind heart often rescued lost animals. The latter got her in hot water sometimes but that never deterred her. Also, that this may have been one of the latter – an IT that someone had abandoned!

So, the three became four – a brother for the two girls, as well as an extra mouth to feed and money for his day care. The arrival of a brother though, was a welcome injection of fun for the two girls. Each day after school, Angela hurried home to play with him. He developed into a cheery little chap dragging himself around on his tummy and pleased to play with his sisters. This was his undoing however, because one afternoon before Babs arrived home to prevent this, he moved to greet three errant piglets from next door. They had dug a space below the adjoining fence to explore and to visit on the doorstep. The little one touched the snout of one of the piglets. A few days later his mouth became infected and he was unable to swallow unless his mouth was first cleared of mucus. He became poorly each day unable to fight the infection and Babs resorted to borrowing a few shillings - the current coinage then, to take him to the general hospital back to the city of Georgetown.

This hospital treated people for free but it entailed a lengthy wait, sometimes hours or days and she was unable to leave for refreshment or a drink in case her place in the queue was lost and she would have to resume her wait at the end of it, before being seen by a doctor.

She shifted nearer to the door as the queue moved forward. Hours later she was ushered in and the baby was then admitted to the children's ward. This meant that he would be alone because she needed to return home to the countryside. Babs visited him once, which was all she could afford to do. On her next visit two weeks later, Angela pleaded to accompany her. So, she made that trip with the two girls as far as her youngest sister's home where the younger child of five was left. She would not have been able to walk the distance to the hospital. She would be collected later for their return by train to their home in the countryside.

Angela was with her, as they entered to find the baby looking pale, dull eyed, but with a measure of delight to see them. There was hope in his eyes. When Babs asked a passing nurse if and when the baby had been fed, she received a cursory – 'I don't know' and a shrug. No staff seemed interested to know if the child had been fed. Babs got angry, so she gathered him out of his cot, blanket and all and proceeded to walk out. This prompted staff to pay attention and they attempted to stop her, but she ignored them. Her child was hungry and in need of nursing care but none of them seemed to be bothered.

Angela remembered that fateful day many years later. It had left her traumatised for sixty-two years, well into her sixties until God instilled His healing power to remind her of that incident. That was the moment God had decided that she should remember, and her healing should begin. Until then that incident had gone from her memory. She was eight when this had happened. Babs had walked aimlessly with the sick child on that hot muggy day. Angela noted her mother's silent sobbing but remained silent not quite comprehending the urgency of the situation. Then her mother suddenly veered away from the direction of her sister's home towards her former family doctor's surgery. It was a serene cool waiting room full of patients, therefore the child would be last in that queue. The doctor emerged to beckon another patient in. When he recognised Babs and noted the listlessness of the child on her lap, he called her in.

That kind, generous old man gave the child his first dose of medicine, and the bottled remainder without charge to take with her for later. His instruction was to administer another dose as soon as she had reached her destination. However, he had warned her that the child was in a bad way but had accepted a little of the medication he had given him.

On arrival at her sister's home, it was time to administer the second dose, so Babs settled him as comfortably as she could on her lap and fed him his meds from a teaspoon. He swallowed it, then turned his head to smile at each of the cousins and aunt who had gathered around. He next turned his gaze on Angela's younger sister. She was his close friend. They played together when Angela was at school. She smiled and briefly managed to hold his hand, but when he looked at Angela and did not receive any particular response a brief frown crossed his forehead. Then his gaze focused on his mother's face and lifting his free hand, he gently touched her on the cheek. As his hand dropped, he closed his eyes forever.

Angela was at a loss to see everyone crying, she could not understand why they would weep when he was only asleep. Surely, he will awaken to feel better; he had taken the medication had he not? Her mother explained gently that he would not waken; he had gone. A stunned and later angry Angela stood speechless. There were no tears, they were wrong she told herself angrily. Her anger was directed at herself because she never said goodbye. No one had prepared her for such an outcome and that incident would return to torment her many years later.

At the point of his death the uncle emerged and declared with derision: 'Well, that is the best thing that could happen. Now – she- Babs can concentrate on looking after the other two.' That did it. Angela had never liked that cruel religious leader of his community. He was harsh and cruel to the children and to his wife. Now, Angela decided that she hated him altogether. They would clash later before his untimely death, but she would not miss him. He went briskly to work to order his older sons to make a casket from whatever timber that was available. That same afternoon her eleven- month-old brother was buried. As was the custom, only males were allowed to be present at an interment. Babs never knew where her son was buried, she was told to leave it alone and it was done.

Those seeds of hate and distrust would grow and impel her to flee from it all for fear of what she would become; a revengeful person. Anger turned to hate, and thoughts of revenge planted a growing forest with bitter tasting fruit within her. Babs and her two children were now allowed to return to the family. The disgrace she had given birth to was now gone, they would allow her association with her family. Here, Angela added that the perpetrator of that violation was sent to the UK for his own safety – from whom she could not say or never knew. He was a man- someone of value in that culture, Babs however was not. Women were easily replaced. They were of little value but were needed to be fertile cows who were to be kept supplied with the necessities to produce and to provide all care. Many years passed and Angela learned from a cousin who had herself emigrated to the UK, that the man had died alone in a dirty flat in Scotland. He who is patient receives a just reward.

Chapter One
The meeting

In 1966 a contingent of the British Armed Forces was sent to Guyana, that former British colony, to quell sporadic riots and outbreaks of lawless behaviour. The soon-to-be twenty-one -year old Angela met Francis one evening during a celebration. There was little interaction between them. He was the minibus driver for the evening apparently and he was instructed to drop people off at specific homes.   However, Francis had made a point of leaving Angela to the last. An intrigued Angela was eventually taken to her allocated address with no explanation as to why he had passed her home once and seemed reluctant to take her home. Recollection of that event was that he may have been devising a plan to use her for his future purpose.   It was a complete surprise for her when he had proposed just two months later.

At that time, Angela had been contemplating the possibility of leaving Guyana because of family pressure among other problems.   This came to fruition when she inadvertently learned that her mother was coerced into seeking a suitable bridegroom for her daughter.   It was simply a case of her Mum being compelled to oblige and agree with someone chosen within the religion. A forlorn and desperate Angela had formed a secret plan to save some of her earnings for a one-way ticket to Trinidad where she may be able to live.

The insurance company which employed her was considering opening a branch in Trinidad and would need staff. She was bold enough to approach her boss to consider her for a post there. He had also remembered her since she was a schoolchild because he had caught her scrumping fruit from his fruit tree and had rescued her. School bullies had demanded she gather the fruit for them. She had been dropping only green or partly ripened fruit for them and they hissed threats at her which she, of course, ignored. The bullies ran off, when the Alsatians appeared at the foot of the thorny tree, preventing her from making her escape. The owner had called off the dogs and waited for her to descend and to leave with all the ripe fruit. He was a kind chap and fortunately for her, later became her boss.

The arranged marriage culture and its do-as-you-are-told religious system had made her mother's life as a single parent miserable for years. She had changed under extreme pressures to conform or go without. No longer was she the fun-loving outgoing woman who had taught the young Angela to sing, read and write. Babs had undergone a complete personality change. She became totally short-tempered, vetting Angela's every movement, and reacting negatively to gossip concerning Angela's behaviour and attire. Once again it was that gossipy aunt telling tales.

When Babs was not satisfied with Angela's response to her accusations, she would at times resort to appearing at Angela's workplace to "have a quiet word with whoever was in charge, to keep an eye on Angela". It made Angela then twenty, feel stifled, angry and needing to get away to somewhere, anywhere. No doubt her mother would be left behind to be blamed for not bringing up her daughter properly. It seemed also that Babs had forgotten her own demise as a young woman who felt obliged to enter an unsuitable marriage. Angela had overheard her mother swear that she would never allow her children to be in such a position ever. Short memory or browbeaten into submission?

Angela wanted opportunities for further education, and subsequently to be in a more secure position to choose a career. She liked the sciences and desperately wanted to follow in that field. She had a taste of secondary education when a relative in the UK had paid her college fees for two semesters, but that was cut short when he got into financial difficulty. So, the offer to leave Guyana with Francis for an opportunity to develop herself seemed like a gift. This raised doubts though that her mother would not agree to her marrying outside of their religion.

She was now the only earner enabling them to live in the better, more secure home of Babs's widower cousin. He needed the rent to keep the home running. Angela's earnings also provided money for her sister's further education. There was little left for Angela after her mother demanded she hand it all over. But the shrewd Angela withheld a little for herself. She had gone many years without proper meals or even meals, and when one of her shoes had split on the inside middle upper, her mother told her to "make it do". She needed the money for other things.

What she had overlooked anyway, was the cultural stigma which her elders would deem as bringing disgrace and shame on the family. Therefore, they would readily agree to the idea of Angela marrying a soldier if she left Guyana. Her association with the man from a different religion meant that she had condemned herself through association and needed to be gone from the small community. So, Francis got his way to marry her even though, emigrating would cut short her sister's higher education. Their Mum suffered for years dependent on bits and bobs of handouts from relatives. The three were treated like beggars, outcasts wherever they were able to find shelter. Her sister would be forced to leave education and to seek employment, for herself and their mother to continue to live at that proper address.

Menial work only lasted for short periods for Babs, and poverty increased its stranglehold on them. When the children were small Babs tried her hand at selling pastries, sandwiches and snacks to office workers in the city. This meant getting up early to cook and see to the children. There was no one to babysit or no family member to leave the two children with. At the age of three Angela and her baby sister were shut in the back of a shop for the entire day while Babs walked several miles to sell her stuff. Occasionally, an aunt would sneak away from her dominant husband on the pretext of going to the nearby market, but brought a little morsel for Angela and perhaps change the baby's nappy, give her a little milk and then rush off. Even Ivan, Aunt Betty's eldest son who was then nine, was sent by his mum after school to keep the two company until Babs's return. It was Aunt Betty's second marriage and her then husband resented the idea of caring for Ivan therefore it was safe for him to remain out of sight.

Chapter Two
Marriage

Francis had the Army visit Angela's home to interview her about her suitability and intentions to leave Guyana. A few irrelevant questions came then she was asked if she had any children to declare. *Deja' vu!* The unsuspecting Angela was unaware that this was not protocol but Francis's way of ensuring she would be entirely dependent on him, away from any interference from her relatives. She had no way of knowing that this would be a pattern of his isolation for her.

Their brief time, two months to be exact, as a couple allowed Angela a glimpse of Francis's lack of concern for her. A day at the seaside turned out to be a near miss with death for Angela. The teenage fashion craze at that time was bikinis and Angela, not wishing to be different, got herself a pretty blue checked one although she couldn't swim. When they arrived at the beach the group of three or four couples, were engrossed in the initial preparation to set up blankets to sit and relax or eat when, without warning, Francis lifted Angela and ran down the beach towards the incoming tide.

Her alarm and protests were ignored. He did not believe that she was unable to swim. She recalled being let go of as he threw her into the Atlantic Ocean but had no recollection of how long she had been in the water. She was startled to find herself on the blanket and the group stood watching as she was resuscitated. He never apologised but simply said he thought that she could swim. It was her first near death experience even before she would marry him.

Their wedding day was a bit of a fiasco for Angela. She had involved herself in preparations for the event with an air of detachment. It was a kind of excitement for her, until the actual day arrived. Her lovely Aunt Beth who had taught her secretarial skills arrived and did her hair and makeup. A jeweller uncle gave her a pair of beautiful silver drop earrings with matching necklace, along with his best wishes. Another seamstress Aunt Beatrice made her full wedding dress and her entire trousseau. All Angela needed to do was to purchase materials then design her outfits and they were made to fit within a few weeks.

That initial anticipation continued up to her arrival at the church. She had lovely things to wear, family to oversee her preparations and no worry except for her Mum who remained quietly in the background throughout.

Her favourite Uncle Harry who was employed at the airport was to give her away, but he was urgently needed on her wedding day and a seventeen-year-old student John stood in. John was the only one with a suit, so the job fell to him.

He was a tad nervous, but he did very well. Angela and he had spent a couple of hours practising the slow wedding walk into the Catholic church. When they arrived on the day, however, Angela had the collywobbles and forgot all about that walk. She just wanted to get the entire event over and done with as quickly as possible.

When the priest, a mere three years older than her groom, asked that crucial question – 'Do you take this man...' Angela completely lost her voice. No sound came as she opened her mouth, absolutely nothing, not even a tiny squeak. The priest discreetly passed over to the next procedure. It was all surreal for her. He hurriedly concluded the ceremony to satisfy the guest-filled pews and ushered bride and groom into the vestry for the signing. Angela was grateful for that respite which allowed her time to regain her composure. The priest commiserated with her, adding that such situations happened occasionally therefore he was able to sympathise and help ease her numbed feeling. Many years later during a disagreement, Francis reminded her of the oath she had made and she was able to counteract with no – she had been unable to make that oath because she had lost her voice.

Photographs were taken on the church's front steps and then the wedding procession left the church to cross the road to the building opposite for the reception. To their left the cricket Test match was also over, and the wedding guests saw the spectators emerging from a side gate to proceed in the wedding party's direction. When they saw the bridal procession, they all set about shouting congratulations, clapping and cheering. Angela though was still in her surreal state, she was aghast at all that attention and hurried up the stairs to the privacy of the sports centre. Regaining some control after a brief rest, she circulated and accepted congratulations from everyone, then noted that her mother had arrived earlier with a few sweetmeats. Angela was embarrassed to note that she had intentionally worn an old frock instead of the dress which they had agreed on when they chose the fabric. Ah well, thought Angela, she understood that that was her mother's way of showing her disapproval of the Catholic wedding service.

Traditionally celebratory events in Guyana follow any party: the music played, folk danced and helped themselves from the buffet table as they desired. The buffet was a courtesy gift from the regimental caterers. On this occasion only a few managed to fill their plates in the expectation of replenishing them as the evening progressed. However, when the music stopped for an interval and folk went to the buffet table it was empty. All the food had gone. Angela was mystified and spoke to the soldier who had served it up. He explained that because people did not help themselves previously, he and his colleague assumed that the food was no longer needed and so had dumped the lot.

Oh dear, this must have been an English tradition, the bewildered Angela thought and she then had to explain and apologise to everyone. It was a total disaster, even her toddler flower maid got nothing.. The poor child had carried her basket of flowers and did as she was instructed with no reward of food. All the locals were thoroughly amused at this disaster which left the soldiers red faced.

A few days before the final day in Guyana, the 25th September 1966, it was packing day and their Army-supplied boxes arrived. Angela had more experience of packing because of the twenty-three or more home moves which she was able to recall and so she had set about the task. Then an argument arose when Francis wanted to dump fragile pieces into the wooden case without stuff to cushion them from accidental or freight impacts. It was just a simple difference of opinion, but her mother intervened and told him to slap Angela because of her cheek towards him. Her dominant religious culture again!

That was soon dealt with by a threat from Angela to wreck the place if Francis obeyed. Her mother left them alone, she knew her daughter well enough to know it was not an empty threat. Also, Uncle Etienne whose house it was, interrupted Babs to support Angela, and told her that it was none of her business. Francis though appeared pleased. It seemed that he would receive no objections if and when he chose physically to abuse his wife. On the day Angela departed forever from her home her mother sobbed and tried to hug her, but Angela pushed her away. She did not want any sentimental words; they were false. Once again, she felt rejected and abandoned to her new faraway fate.

Chapter Three
Departure Day

At the improvised check-in desk in the Army camp there was a queue to check and stamp passports and details before boarding the RAF carrier. Angela had her first introduction of racism when her turn for check-in arrived. The soldier shot her a scathing glance and noted on the form: hair black, eyes black. They were both brown, so she deliberately turned his completed form to correct the description. He looked at her and noting the challenging stare she returned, he accepted the form and stamped her passport.

Angela had little time or opportunity for them to become acquainted, so she had to learn after being cut off from familiar surroundings. The RAF carrier stopped briefly in Bermuda to refuel and there Angela experienced a panic attack, unsure of her decision to marry that stranger. In a bit of a panic, she locked herself in the airport's washroom with a silly hope that the plane would continue without her. After about half an hour she tentatively emerged to see her new husband and the pilot pacing back and forth as they waited for her. Francis approached her and hissed, 'where the b... y hell, were you?' The shaking but defiant Angela replied, 'oh, I got locked in the washroom.' Throughout their marriage, he would refer to that incident as an example of her stupidity, but she never told him the truth. Let him think whatever makes him feel clever. Angela, in that moment of panic, wanted to be left on that island. She had no desire to live in the UK.

From Bermuda the carrier flew into its first electrical storm which caused it to drop two or three times to about five hundred feet at each drop. Passengers gasped in fear and held their breath for the next drop. Angela became twenty-one on that day, 26th September 1966. She had stupidly hoped that they would be forced to land and then she may be able to run away. Alas, it didn't. The carrier eventually touched down in Newfoundland for refreshments and lunch courtesy of the regiment. It was a beautiful day, a little cloudy at intervals but inside the airport which had wide viewing windows, it was warm.

Angela had never had a meal of more than one course and after having her soup she rose to venture outside because it had begun to snow, and she needed some fresh air. When she explained her intention, Francis laughed and said that was only the first course. Oh dear, an impatient Angela ate as quickly as she was able to leaving most of her salad and declining the sweet without asking what that would be. Without more preamble she excused herself and headed outside where it had continued to snow. It felt beautiful, soft snowflakes unfortunately melting as they landed. She paid no attention to the fact that her peach linen sleeveless two-piece suit wasn't meant for these conditions. She enjoyed that brief feeling of freedom, the fresh clean air in her lungs and a short time of pure joy.

From Newfoundland the carrier finally landed at ten thirty on a late September evening, at Grosvenor Airport in Northern Ireland. At the check-in desk Angela's own case was opened to reveal a surprise; Francis had hidden two large bottles of what he had stated as cooking oil but were in fact rum. Thankfully, the desk clerk was keen to be rid of them at that time of night, so he allowed it. He even allowed Angela to have all her gold jewellery even any extra pieces which were normally checked. The convoy left for Hollywood Barracks and family quarters in County Down.

Their allocated ground floor flat was stark, cold and very uninviting for someone arriving at night from the warmth of the tropics. That place never got warmer, with only a fireplace in the front room and green lino on the floors. Francis would not allow Angela to buy rugs. The cold walls were only painted therefore there was little to resist the cold. Before they left Northern Ireland, he had insisted on inviting his mother and sister to visit for a week. Angela had her misgivings because of the cold room they were expected to share on the shaded side of the building, but she was told by Francis that would not be a problem for them. It was and she would be forever dubbed as neglectful and unable to cook. This latter ability was true anyway more so in preparing English-style meals. She especially recalled how Francis had dictated they had duck a l' orange for their first Christmas meal. Angela agreed, but only if he made it so she may observe. Anyway, they eventually had roast lamb that was easier!

Following a miscarriage months later she conceived again soon after and the following year – 1968 – their first child was breach born in a hospital in Dundonald, County Down. This was a little amusing experience to remember. In their married quarters Angela had alerted Francis that her waters had broken, and he in his panic had rushed out to the nearest telephone booth two to three blocks away to call for an ambulance. He was butt naked, but thankfully it was the early hours of the morning so no one was about. She went into labour in the hospital and was medicated to ease the pain which resulted in her being vaguely aware of the rest of the procedure. Angela was not used to pain medication and found that it incurred drowsiness or just knocked her out, but she was urged by nurses to accept it. She lay in her hospital bed for five days without seeing her child or her husband. He had gone with the regiment's rugby team to play in Guernsey on the same morning that she was admitted for delivery and had forgotten to tell his wife.

Staff changed shifts but had never once enquired if she had seen or held her daughter until day five when the observation nurse remarked how beautiful the baby was. The nurse was surprised that no one had bothered to show Angela her baby. An hour later Angela was at last wheeled to view the baby from a glass-topped viewing corridor. She was in an incubator because she was a little underweight. Francis arrived on that same afternoon's visit as well and it was only then his neglected wife learned why he had not visited. Angela had miscarried their first child and by way of sympathy Francis had told her not to worry there… would be plenty more later. She said to herself that was not going to happen.

Chapter Four
Posted to the UK.

She was aware that the regiment was due to return to the UK and therefore was not surprised when barely a few weeks after giving birth that day arrived. She was apprehensive.   The couple moving would not be a problem but now she had a young child, and no forward accommodation was available on departure from Northern Ireland. Therefore, Francis took Angela and new baby to stay with his mother in Middlesex which he had assured her would not be a problem for his mother. Declaring that his wife and child were in suitable temporary accommodation, the allocations officer would then focus on others who were in more urgent need.

Unfortunately, his mother was not pleased on their arrival and had insisted that she needed the spare room for her eldest daughter's visit 'sometime soon', and she reminded him that he had not asked for permission before appearing. He was absolutely certain that his mother would not object. Angela had repeatedly urged him for months to contact her and he had lied and said that he had done so. It would be all right; his mother would not mind he reassured her. He had lied to Angela, exactly why she never knew, but it had made her feel uncomfortable that she had imposed their presence on his mother. He had an inflated ego. He became male head of the family he had informed Angela, when his father had passed away. After the Second World War his father had returned home a shrapnel-wounded war veteran soldier who died a short time later.

Going to that flat was a bad move, an embarrassing situation which only grew worse. His mother regarded Angela as an inconvenience and an alien. She pretended to be 'helpful' although she declared that she was unable to understand Angela when she spoke. As soon as Francis returned to his unit, she had set about criticising Angela on everything and anything: her accent, her mention of her native foods, questions about what kind of meals and foods were served in Guyana, before dismissing it 'as no longer required to eat nonsense'. She corrected her when she forgot to use 'us' instead of 'my', and even to feeding the baby on proper English baby's milk – which was not good because the baby was unable to digest milk especially full creamed. In fact, his mother bought a tin of what she considered her grandchild should be fed. The first feed was spewed out within minutes and at this the mother-in-law conceded as the baby cried with hunger.

Weeks went by and this charged situation continued. She tried to urge Francis on each weekend visit to check if accommodation could be considered but he had constantly told her nothing could be done, as it was up to the allocations officer. Angela felt lost. She had no one to confide her distress to, except when Francis visited. So, tension grew and she began to despair. How long must she keep silent and endure endless criticism? It seemed that nothing she did or not do incurred criticism. Angela was a primitive who she needed to educate and reform into English ways. Angela was not used to being served side vegetables which tasted very bland anyway so consequently she left most of this and incurred the annoyance of mother–in-law. After gaining Angela's trust to ask what greens she would like – Angela had a mound of cabbage almost every day. She longed for green beans, ochroes and spinach but no it had to be cabbage or peas. She still dislikes peas.

Her mother-in-law began to bake one day but saw that there was not enough sugar. Angela quickly offered to visit the nearby high street shop to buy some. This would allow her time to breathe in the outside air, she surmised. She set off and made the purchase then walking with heavy footsteps on the return she started to daydream and before she had noticed she was well past the corner to the flat. A frantic Angela became anxious. She had no idea how far her steps had led her. She asked directions from a couple of passers-by and hastily retraced her way back to the flat to a furious mother-in-law. She was told that she was incapable of even the simplest task of going to the shop. Angela became silent and endured the demeaning tirade, it was no use she told herself the woman was not sympathetic to her situation at all. She never told Francis what had happened.

Then, one weekend his youngest sister also stayed over. Francis told Angela that he would speak with his mother on Angela's behalf. However, Angela was not to be present at this discussion. 'It was a family matter,' he told her. Oh, was Angela an outsider then? More like another warning arrow. She never heard what was discussed but washed the baby's laundry as she was advised to occupy herself, in the tiny galley kitchen. She heard a kerfuffle, then his sister stormed in to accuse a startled Angela that she was the cause of their mother being physically abused by Francis. Angela was speechless: what had she said to him that would incur such behaviour?

The tension became worse until eventually Francis visited and announced that the Army had found temporary accommodation for them, in a disused camp in Swindon. Most of the families were allocated quarters in Warminster where the regiment was based. It was a welcome and grateful break. The neglected house needed a lot of cleaning inside and out but Angela didn't mind. During the summer she loved to hear the cuckoos hidden in the overgrown field in the front of the house. The site was remote. Only a handful of families were temporarily housed there but not too close to each other. Shops were very far on buses, but the local post office provided most essentials and even delivered them.

Whilst at his mother's flat on a weekend visit, he took Angela and baby to his godmother's home. This was the first individual to treat Angela as a person. This kind, elderly lady warned him to treat Angela with respect and that he must behave – it seemed then to the naive Angela that this lady knew him well. When he returned to barracks and Angela had the opportunity to visit her again, she expanded her remarks with more warnings for Angela to be careful, not to allow Francis to misbehave. Angela was able to relax and to chat with her and her neighbour friend quite easily.

On that follow-up visit, Angela thought to relate to her an amusing tactic of Francis. He pretended to obey his mother's instruction to attend Mass on Sunday visits. With his wife alongside he would set out for the bus to church, but he had other ideas to occupy the time until they returned home for Sunday lunch. One such Sunday they had alighted from the bus – to church, at least two stops before. A baffled

Angela did wonder why. He turned into a nearby road and went directly to one particular house. At his knock a pretty young woman stood somewhat startled and with a degree of visible apprehension.

He pointedly asked to be invited in, which she did – possibly because Angela was with him. In her living room, he asked for a cuppa and though still apprehensive she obliged. Within seconds after she had left the room he rose and told Angela to wait while he would help with preparing the tea. He also made a point of closing the room door. Angela sat alone and waited.

That tea never came and Angela was about to go in search of them because it took so long, when he suddenly and a bit hastily appeared with a stony expression and announced that they must leave The girl was almost immediately behind and seemed agitated but relieved, and had both arms up in a defensive position, Angela noticed how she had moved one hand to gently rub her other lower arm. Angela said her goodbye and went past her to the front door. The girl then stepped aside to allow him to pass, but Francis had deliberately hovered until Angela was out of earshot and then said something to the silent girl as she held her front door ready to close it behind them. The door was hastily closed behind him.

Angela noted that the girl never smiled. She merely maintained a look of apprehension throughout. As they walked away Angela asked who the girl was. She had assumed her to be another relative, but he made a dismissive gesture with his hand and said she was someone from his youthful days. Angela was silent not quite sure how to take that.

When his godmother heard this account, she expressed her alarm and revealed that he was engaged to that girl, but the girl had returned his ring after just one day. Clever girl that! Angela was sorry that the poor, startled girl had to endure more of his bullying. She was alone in that house and therefore very vulnerable to a bully such as Francis. It was hoped that he would not return to harass her because that was how he operated. No woman would be allowed to say no to him. Angela loved visiting his godmother with whom she was able to relax and chat with.

The opportunity for a follow-up visit never happened because his godmother herself visited his mother's home a few days before they left for their accommodation in Swindon. Angela never got her address or full name, his mother avoided Angela's request for this or if was given to Francis to pass on to Angela she never received it. With his godmother's final warning for her to be careful and a regret that Angela would be moving far away and she would not be able to see her or her child, she gave Angela a lengthy hug, and a rag doll that she had made for the baby and with a degree of urgency she told Angela to look after herself. Those warnings would materialise over the couple's thirteen years of unsettling family life and their distant relationship.

They spent a few months in that temporary accommodation in Swindon until they were allocated a flat in Warminster. It was an end middle flat and the end walls again were cold, it was open to the cold winds which blew against the building and the second bedroom which was to be used for their year-old first child would be covered in green mould that had to be removed every three weeks. The toddler developed an extreme bout of gastro-enteritis.

Francis told her not to turn the underfloor heating on because it was expensive, so during the day the flat became icy cold. Cheryl, the one-year-old, sat on the chilly floor every day and played with Angela's kitchen bowl and wooden spoon. It made a noise, so it was a good toy. Perhaps she had contracted a severe tummy cold which dehydrated her and the Army GP visited daily to check on the toddler's progress. Angela borrowed a couple of mobile electric heaters to warm the sick child's room unknown to Francis and these were returned each afternoon before he arrived home. It was the only means of keeping the toddler's temperature down as her skin became opaque and loose to touch. The GP was concerned. It was a worry sometimes to try to keep her alive in those stark conditions.

Angela had also given birth to another child and this one slept in the same bed with her and Francis or in a cot in the living room. The doctor had advised her to keep the children apart to avoid cross-infection. Francis would not allow Angela to turn the heating on during the day therefore she needed to improvise or juggle and dress the little ones in lots of warm things. Keeping them apart was stressful and Angela became anxious for the health of both of them. Francis though was too occupied within his unit. He was being allowed opportunities to move up in rank.

Angela got pregnant eight months after the birth of the first child, because she was refused any contraceptives by the Army doctor. He had dismissed her request saying to her that that was what one married for, to have children and that he could not give her any contraceptive unless her husband authorised it. Angela, returned to ask Francis to accompany her on her next visit to ask again, but Francis refused; that's not his problem he had said, they were women's issues, and he was not interested. Yet, he was overheard explaining to his visiting mate in their flat one day; "the silly b...h got pregnant again I don't know how that happened." Well, if he didn't know, how should his wife?

The policy during the Seventies was that married women needed the consent of their spouses before contraceptives would be issued. Also, if the couple were reluctant to have more than two children, they were refused sterilisation until they had a third child. Angela was aware of her husband's reticent attitude towards children and was desperate to prevent any future disagreements regarding that issue but the powers that be dictated otherwise regardless of possible consequences, especially so in unstable marriages and Francis and Angela's marriage was definitely in this category.

They moved from place to place into Army-leased properties or into family camps almost every ten months or so. At those times Angela, who did much of the packing anyway, was able to put her youthful packing and moving skills into practice. He was in training for promotion most of the time (possibly to compensate for his demotion before his marriage). Where there were mixed regiments or affiliated personnel occupying the same married quarters, it was sometimes difficult to have friends especially if his regiment would be the last to be accommodated because they were scattered. Families or couples were given accommodation when and where it became available. Though it was always away from civilians, this was for security purposes really. It was the regiment's responsibility to provide for their soldiers and families.

Thirteen years of short-term homes away from civilians and observing security restrictions because of the IRA, was not so bad except for the two children's education which stopped and restarted each time they had moved. Cheryl, the older child, grumbled. She enjoyed her time at school. Denise, the second daughter, didn't care. She had little interest in education. Her assurance was that her Dad loved her and therefore she would be secure. Her school reports consistently stated that she would do better if she paid attention. However, Dad reassured her that it was okay. There was no need to worry.

Chapter Five
In Germany

A first posting to Germany when the girls were almost three and a half and four, took them to a more sturdily erected block of flats in Westphalia – much warmer indoors than those in the UK. At once, Angela noticed that Francis gained more confidence as soon as they arrived. He was on familiar territory. The regiment was previously stationed there before his marriage, but family quarters may have been unfamiliar for him as a single bloke. To him, it was like resumption of his secretive lifestyle with new and familiar like-minded folk within and outside the army. However, this time he had a wife and family and had been promoted and therefore needed to be more careful to retain that aura of respectability that seemed to be so very important to him. That adage that leopards never change their spots is true.

Angela recalled an embarrassing visit when she had first arrived in the UK. Francis took her to show her some of the places of interest in London – a bit wasted on her though. He had taken her up a flight of stairs where a doorman remonstrated with him. He demanded entrance to the place and was reluctantly allowed in. Angela immediately felt uncomfortable as unwelcome looks were directed at her, but Francis boldly ordered tea for her and whisky for himself. Angela sat with her back to the few bedecked uniformed men who milled around with and without a glass in their hand, but they did not engage in any conversation with Francis as he sat facing them. He acknowledged a couple of the men and they nodded in return only. She was relieved to leave that stuffy, dismal environment to the preeners who may have felt just as relieved to see the couple go. That appeared to Angela as a deliberate act of defiance on his part which was pointless to her.

Although Francis relished his newfound aura of respectability he would not then be able to overtly resume his old habits. It was easy to ignore any consequences before with his carefree lifestyle. He would have had the Army to protect him from any after-effects. The Army's expectation of his behaviour would inhibit him, so too would his wife. Therefore, he began to condition her to conform to his lifestyle and to become a participant in whatever he was involved in outside of work. If she was to accept and become a partner to whatever he wanted then he would be able to blame her for any problems which may arise: his partner in his seedy practices and a perfect alibi.

She seemed to be reluctant however, a thorn in his side, resisting his half-baked attempts to mould her to his desires. Since he seemed to fail in those attempts, he therefore decided that she may respond to pressure to conform to his way of life if he had help from another female. This was where he enlisted the assistance of an odious couple. They were his friends and had agreed to his request to help Angela. It was not him who needed help. It was Angela. She was the unreasonably stubborn one and he explained to them that she had mental health problems. Unfortunately for him, Angela was a lot more shrewder and appeared to be always a step ahead of his half-baked schemes. He was inept at planning or thinking things through. Even, his motor transport examination which he was familiar with caused him to vacillate. For Angela, life with Francis would forever be on high alert, not because of the IRA but because of his behaviour.

After an argument one day, in the confines of their bathroom, she had refused to accompany him to the flat of Mr and Mrs Odious and he became angry. To demonstrate that he was boss he had slapped her on the face. Angela retaliated with the tail comb in her hand and he fled. She was livid and he knew it. She approached the families' officer about leaving him to return to the UK. Francis agreed, but only if she agreed to seek psychiatric help. Though she agreed to this she had no intention of doing so. He drove out of the camp but held on to her passport and pretended to head towards the airport. Instead, he had turned into a field in which there was a small windmill and then had switched the engine off.

The control freak begun to exert pressure with a threat, an ultimatum issued in a crook's measured tones. She was ordered to behave, not to leave him, or to cause disgrace to him or to his family. If she insisted on leaving, he would strangle her right there. Not in the least scared by this tactic, although she noted he was blind with rage and capable of carrying out his threat, she countered, 'Oh yes and how will you explain my murder?' 'That's easy, I will explain that we were arguing and things got out of hand'. The law must be pretty silly, Francis!

Yes, he was dumb enough to follow through that threat. She laughed and said, 'okay I'll leave it for another time then.' The fool accepted this and assumed he had won. He would return to the FO to say that 'she had come to her senses'.

Francis had actually throttled Angela before – it was yet another refusal to comply with his order to accompany him to the odious couple's flat. They kept strange civilian company and wanted to use Angela who had acquired a limited knowledge of German for their activities. So, Francis flew into a rage and grabbed her by the throat and blindly applied pressure until Angela had passed out. This probably caused him to panic so he lifted her on to their bed, closed the curtains and then summoned the doctor to explain how they were arguing when she suddenly passed out.

The doctor, of course, never looked at her throat for bruising but examined her to see if she was pregnant. She was able to hear and see what was happening but was unable to speak and of course Francis stood guard at the foot of the bed watching to ensure that she did not tell that doctor the truth. When the doctor left with instructions that Angela should visit the surgery for a test, Francis returned from seeing the man leave and ordered Angela to get up. She ignored him and took her time recovering. When she was eventually up and was able to speak she told him – 'next time finish the job because it would be a pleasure to see you jailed for life'. He knew that she meant every word, so he stormed out of their flat on some pretence and returned later in the evening.

Aware of his intention to kill her made her contemplate her children's future. She knew that he did not want the responsibility of looking after children and suspected that he would dump them with family or put them into care, but she would not allow him to do that. No, she would try to be patient and then act but not outside the UK. She had no means or knowledge where to seek trusted advice. Any legal enquiries would be filtered back to him anyway, and Francis was a devious man, a brutal soldier who put into practice what he was trained to do.

On their return to the UK from Westphalia, the regiment was stationed in Bulford Camp, in Hampshire.   As they left Germany for the UK Angela learned that there was another child brewing in her womb. This one would be UK born as was the second.

Angela felt daily exhausted and was unaware that this feeling was a result of a leaky gas fire which had affected her and the girls. Each day after school the eldest, Cheryl sat with her back to the gas fire to watch their favourite children's programmes on the television as their Mum did the tea. One day when the children were at school Angela was summoned by telephone – relayed by a soldier in the main barracks - and informed by the school to visit the hospital immediately because one of the children had been behaving oddly and out of character. The teachers became concerned and had sent her off to the nearby hospital. It was the child who used to sit with her back to the leaky gas fire. She had gas inhalation poisoning.

The third child, Emma, then two and at home with Angela - had to be pushed in her buggy to the hospital a mile away. The sick child was in a ward on the second floor and this meant ascending with the buggy an outer long flight of steps up to the second-floor small landing. As she opened the door, she was confronted by a haughty nurse who told her not to bring the young child into the hospital as it was not allowed. So how would Angela be able to see Cheryl who had apparently been admitted? Thankfully, that archaic rule had gone. 'Well, you will have to return alone'. 'No,' insisted Angela, 'I need to visit my child who is in there.' There was a brief pause from the stiff-necked woman, then, 'We will allow you five minutes to see your child but you must leave the younger one outside.' So Angela had to leave the toddler strapped in her buggy on the small landing before she was allowed in to see the eldest child of seven, but only for five minutes. She was warned again, as it was past visiting time. There are names for such idiots.

The anxious Angela was angry and on her way out of the grounds she approached the first soldier who chanced by to telephone Francis in Northern Ireland to sort out the stupid situation. If she was unable to find someone to babysit or look after the toddler then she would not be able to visit the hospital. Nor would she know when her daughter would be discharged. There was no telephone at home. The message to visit that hospital was delivered by a soldier from their barracks on the opposite side of the families' quarters, which was across the main road in Tidworth. It was absolute bloody-mindedness in that hospital with its archaic rules. They dismissed her as if she was irrelevant. Only they knew how to look after the child.

Somehow that poor soldier saw the state Angela was in and used the sentry's payphone with his own coins to telephone the regiment in Northern Ireland. He explained the situation briefly then handed Angela the phone to elaborate. Francis was granted emergency leave for two days to sort things out. He brought their seven-year-old home from the hospital. No explanation was given to Angela, but she was relieved. The school contacted her later to check on the child.

It was only when the child was returned to resume her lessons that Angela learned that their daughter's behaviour was erratic. She was laughing uncontrollably and spoiling the meals of her fellow pupils. It was soon after when Angela herself begun to feel tired and irritable and when a gas engineer called to service the fire that week, she learnt that the fire had a leak. It had been recently changed to natural gas which masked any smell. She and the children were slowly being gas poisoned. Being at home throughout the day meant that she was exposed to the poisonous effects for a long while.

About a week after this palaver, Francis had returned home from Northern Ireland. One evening he sat and indulged in his sports programme while Angela sat reading. After they had retired Francis began to argue with her about something trivial, at which she had disagreed, and he became angry. She rose to get a drink. The gas continued to affect her, and she tried to end the argument, but he assumed that she was ignoring him. He followed her down the stairs, when a weary Angela told him that it would be better to end the marriage because there was a decided absence of unanimity amongst everything else in their marriage.

At this, he became furious that she had dared to speak to him in that way. He stripped her just inside their front door and told her with a snarl to: 'Go now, you come with nothing so you take nothing.' She stood silent unmoving and feeling completely exhausted, while he threatened to shove her out of the door naked to be exposed to the barracks opposite. She continued to stand there until the following morning. Next day, he redressed her and led her by her arm to the GP's surgery a block away.

This was an odd visit in more ways than she expected. The elderly female GP, probably too tired herself, looked Angela over, then asked her for her date of birth and announced: 'Oh, this is normal, people born under Angela's birth sign are indecisive.' Ditherers was her expression. Francis said he had brought her there because he believed his wife was on the verge of a nervous breakdown. To which the GP said: 'Anyway dear, I will send you away for a rest because I think that you need a rest.'

Angela, too exhausted to argue, merely responded; at that moment anywhere would be better than being at home with him. Angela was referred to and admitted to a psychiatric unit somewhere. Neither the staff nor Francis would tell her its location. She was there for three weeks. Each week, he left the three children in the care of whoever he was able to persuade to do him a favour, to visit. This was really to persuade her to come home. Heck no, she thought she was away from him and will try to savour this enforced but restricted freedom.

She had refused any psychiatric assessment and proposed treatment offered. The staff tried to convince her to accept treatment, but she had steadfastly refused. There was nothing wrong with her other than fatigue and she took the opportunity to rest. Eventually however, she conceded because a lesbian patient began to pester her. She did not want more problems to deal with; her home life had ample supplies of problems. On her return, she noted how forlorn Emma appeared. She had been refusing food and had probably felt abandoned – she must have been ill-treated wherever he had left her, an unwanted young child to hamper the person's routine. There was also a degree of hostility towards her from nearby families on her return. Goodness knows what explanation he had given them.

Angela used his contrition to suggest that she needed to occupy herself whilst he was away in Northern Ireland. A part-time job would help. She knew that he did not want her to have any independence but maybe she would be less anxious. So, he persuaded the woman at a tailoring and repairs shop on the edge of the barracks for his wife to work on the machines for a few hours each week. Again, he had orchestrated where he wanted her to be. The youngest at just over two was required to sit strapped into her buggy for up to eight hours, because the floor was covered in pins and other sharp objects and she could not be allowed to walk around the sewing machines because it was unsafe. It was thoroughly against Health and Safety and the place was not warm either.

Such concerns meant nothing to Francis. Angela said she wanted to occupy her time doing something useful. If she refused that opportunity there would never be another one. Angela's earnings amounted to a total of £16 per week and Francis suggested that it be used for housekeeping, while he saved what she would have normally used - £20 - towards a holiday. But they never went on holiday; it was another level of his control. There was no use arguing.

He would soon use another way to divest her of any independence. Well, Angela played the game and withheld her purchase on items which he was asked to pay for. If he complained about the lack of anything she simply told him to buy it himself. He relished the good life and would try to impress her with his taste for costly foodstuff which were useless for young children. So, where there's a way!

Chapter Six
Return to Germany to the same camp.

That second posting to the same camp in Westphalia was almost Angela's fatal demise. First, she had become friendly with a former Trinidadian woman and her family who resided in one of the civilian flats. They had a lot in common to chat about and food to share. This friendship grew until one day when, as arranged, Angela went to visit. She got part way up the drive when the woman opened her door and shouted for Angela to go away. A perplexed Angela stood with her arms opened wide to ask why, what had she done to the woman. Her reply was: 'You know well what you did. He told me everything, don't ever come to my flat again.' Angela was left embarrassed as windows overlooking the driveway had opened and curious heads stuck out. Later, when Angela related this to Francis, she noted that he appeared to be uncomfortable and had avoided looking directly at her, but he merely said: "Forget it, never mind, it's just one of those things." It was not the only time when he had orchestrated her detachment from being too friendly with others nor would it be the last.

Some of the wives close to their flat including nearby blocks got together during the day to socialise in Angela's flat. Until he became aware of this and begun to return home for lunch, on most days he didn't return home to have lunch. If Angela asked what he did or where he went it was a mumble or a feeble excuse. He was curious to know what was discussed in his absence. Then one by one the women disappeared never to visit again.

Angela noticed their absence and joked to her friend opposite: 'Was it something I said?' 'No,' came the surprised reply. 'We love coming to your flat. It was welcoming and we got on well together. However, when Francis came home the women felt uncomfortable because he continually behaved badly or inappropriately touched them. Sorry to tell you this but that was why most of us would not return. Please come to our flat instead because we would like you to.' Angela told Francis about his behaviour soon after and his reply was: 'You are just jealous that I do not give you more attention.' A very thick skinned individual or maybe thick headed!

Oh, he had allowed her to remain friends with the wife of a private in his company. Angela learned to be cautious of what they discussed though. Not because the woman was vindictive in any way, but she may chat to her husband and unwittingly gave ammunition to Francis via the private - her husband. He was the earpiece who repeated to his Colour Sergeant in return for favours. So, Angela kept conversations low key most of the time. Once Francis had warned her not to discuss him in company, he did not like that. Angela though, was angry and countered: 'I am indoors caring for my children and a husband, I have no pastime except to read and even that you tried to deny me so I will discuss you and my children because those are the things which are topical to me.' His mouth pursed with anger but she dared him to react.

She was more than three stones lighter than him and was in reality no match for his thirteen stones, but that had never hampered her before and she was not going to be intimidated continuously. She was really compliant to his stupid demands because she needed to protect her children and she was also aware of her lack of knowledge in unfamiliar surroundings. His attempt at dominance over his wife was more comical than fearful to her.

Angela read most of the series of Denis Wheatley on his psychological crimes. One-night Francis decided to read her current book borrowed from the library and almost scared himself silly. He had sat up to read it because he was restless and unable to sleep. When he had finished the book around one thirty in the morning and rose from the front room naked, to retire, he made a gaffe, and instead of taking one step out of the room to turn to his left towards the bedroom he had instead taken two steps and had come face to face with a long mirror on the adjoining wall. Angela, disturbed by his movement, heard his loud startled exclamation 'Jesus bl...y wept' and she lay stifling her laughter at his stupidity and weakness. It was merely a psychological crime, but that brutish idiot was unable to handle it. How funny!

Being outside of the UK also seemed to embolden him in his efforts to control Angela by any means since she resisted his efforts to pressure her into becoming a partner in his dubious lifestyle. He would devise more and more tactics to inflict fear and insecurity on her. Humiliation failed to reduce her quiet but feisty spirit no matter how hard he tried. Also, most of his efforts to debase her appeared to backfire on him and he was regarded by his comrades and seniors as an idiot, an unfunny comedian. The escalation included incidental or planned ways for her accidental demise. It also offered him opportunities to apologise for his wife's ignorance because she originated from a backward country, he explained.

On that second posting they were allocated a third floor flat. He had enlisted the help of the odious couple to take Angela in hand. The couple with their five-year-old only child had arrived one afternoon for a visit. It was all pre-planned Angela suspected but was to learn why very soon. The woman sat Angela down like a disobedient child and proceeded to explain that if she had someone in mind to leave her husband and children they might be willing to help her. Angela did not know whether to laugh with derision or to cry and with great effort she hopefully applied a woeful expression to lure them falsely into her sense of helplessness. She was handed an A5 piece of paper on which to write to this mysterious person and an envelope was presented for them to post it for her.

Oh corks, thought Angela. What name should she select from her limited knowledge of some bloke far away, out of their reach? She must play along; it was a game that called for quick thinking. She thought up a name to use. A short letter, which was in fact a note, was made up and placed in the presented envelope. Their next move was to wait until she was busy preparing a drink then open and read the note. How obvious!

On her return with the drinks, the woman said to Angela that she should concentrate on her own life here with her husband who loved her - since when! Now that was news. They destroyed the note, drank tea, and left. Francis had hovered in the background as this charade played out, now he emerged to pretend to embrace Angela. She pushed him off and got on with her chores, quietly though she giggled with merriment. If she wanted to contact a secret lover, why would she do that through a third party? How dumb can folk be!

An opportunity for payback came surprisingly quickly when on a chilled autumn evening when the couple were in bed, Francis got up for a bathroom visit. As usual he was naked because he hated pyjamas. As he walked out of their bedroom Angela shot out of bed opened the curtains to the Juliet balcony and flung the doors wide open, then hid behind the bedroom door. The cold air billowed the curtains and chilled the room. He returned and noted the open balcony door and empty bed, then assuming the worst he turned and rushed out of the flat, down to exit the metal door of their block, and around to the back of the building under the balcony. No body! No Angela! Where was she?

Meanwhile, Angela allowed him time to leave the block then rose and locked the flat door and returned briefly to the warmth of their bed. She had closed the curtains and balcony doors. On that evening all the flat occupants had a treat: comedy. He reached upstairs to find himself locked out and began to knock on the door, ringing the bell and begging to be let in. At his persistent whining, doors opened upstairs, middle and lower flats. A brief, 'what's up mate' from a few before they shut their doors exclaiming 'oh sorry mate can't help'. A couple of sniggers or maybe giggles as they exchanged glances with each other from opposite flats. Well, not many married blokes would want to rescue a naked bloke, would they? There were wives and children to consider. Also, the block housed military personnel from different units and regiments and he did not know them.

Angela checked progress at intervals looking through the viewing hole on their door. Outside their flat, Francis stood half bent with his hands full and his rear against the cold wall. The entire entrance way and staircase was glassed from top to bottom with automatic lighting which allowed clear view from the outside. She allowed him about a good thirty minutes or more to be as humiliated as long as possible. Then, anticipating his next move - to rush at the locked door - she stood behind and waited for his rush.

As he stood against the opposite flat door, everyone had gone back to bed to enjoy the pantomime in private. Then, she saw him charge and just at the precise moment opened the door. His momentum took him past the spare room, kitchen and almost into the sitting room and with hands now freed, he skidded to a wobbly stop. Then a surprised (well it worked didn't it?) wife began chiding him, where had he been this time of night without any clothes. She had seen him go out to the bathroom and had expected him to return to their bed. He was red faced and his body well chilled. He started to explain: 'I thought you, oh never mind I am cold' and headed for the warmth of his bed. With a trifle smug and silent titter Angela muttered a comic expression - 'that'll learn ya' and she joined him in bed.

Word of this panto soon spread, and he became the joke of the camp for months after. Give him a taste of what humiliation felt like! Angela's anger at his conniving, oafish behaviour was abated. On visits to the NAAFI, the forces shopping centre, he became renowned and tried to avoid going to shop with Angela. In fact, his notoriety spread farther and longer than expected. He avoided visits to the NAAFI whenever possible and the family visited the Belgium supermarket close by the American PX and as many local supermarkets and other establishments for their monthly shopping.

The girls loved to visit those places, to delight in the wide choice of goodies which were available to them and their food selection also broadened. Angela used those opportunities to secretly add a few items of clothing for the children and the odd selection of something to keep him from grumbling. It was good to spend the tight-fisted git's money for a change. He knew how to mistreat her, but she knew how his small brain worked.

Not all of his behaviour ended well though. Families used to go for drives on a Sunday afternoon to explore and sightsee and also to settle children whose only respite was BFPO school and to remain indoors or within the confines of the families' quartered areas. One such afternoon, Francis suddenly decided to take his family for a drive. Their first delight was as their car had turned a corner at a meander length of road, they were all greeted by the sight of the head of a camel chewing its cud and llamas peering through the high hedged garden.

Further along the road they were on, began a gradual climb, either side obscured by thick, tall bush until it reached the top where there was a short length of a waist high brick and concrete wall. That appeared to be a viewing escarpment with dense bush after the viewing area. The parapet overlooked a wide expanse of parallel lines of barbed and wire fences beyond which stood armed sentries in the distance. A sentry post overlooked that wide area. It was no man's land overlooking East Germany. It was a sheer drop and those sentries instantly trained binoculars on the family.

Francis stopped the car for his family to view the scene and then lifted his two small daughters up on to the parapet to walk back and forth. They assumed this was an exciting play area. Angela however, stood frozen with fear. She was aware how the girls argued and knew that it was Francis who had himself divided them. Children are not aware of danger and this was the most dangerous act from their father. They shoved past each other in excitement while Angela held her breath. When she attempted to coax them down Francis pushed her aside. A car sounded its horn in alarm two or three times as it passed by, but Francis turned and laughed before returning his attention to the girls. Angela dared not look away. She was so cold with fear. Eventually, the older one, Cheryl, moved towards her and Angela managed to lift her down to safety. The younger would not have listened to Angela so she had to just watch in horror.

Angela had no recollection of the remainder of that day and her fear remained with her throughout that night until the following afternoon. It had revealed the danger that their children were in and the inability of Francis to understand the feelings of anyone but himself. He lacked any feeling, empathy or understanding of and for others, he treated them all and his exploits as adventures. Accidents or consequences he would explain as 'just one of those things'. She resolved to try to protect the girls as much as she was able to in whatever time she was allowed to.

Francis's next attempt to stage an accident for her would arise when the Major left his Rover in Francis's care because he needed to return to the

UK on urgent business. Francis reverted to his teenage blue suede shoes gang days of being loutish and impatient to stand still. He was agog with the excitement to drive that posh car. The Rover was brought and parked in the small parking area close to their block. Angela noted his excitement and was unaware of the Rover in Francis's care until he said that he wanted her to go for a drive with him to the Mohne Zee Dam. The family had already visited it one Sunday afternoon but then the girls had become tired of walking and they had all left for home. This was not planned and Angela wondered what the urgency was?

She needed someone to check on the sleeping children anyway. Francis told her that the children should be all right and that they would not be more than an hour at the most. She was aware of Francis's idea of an hour and insisted on asking someone to check on the children whilst they slept. He lacked any sense of responsibility, so it was often left to her to ensure that their children were safe. He was impatient to get going, so the wife from the opposite flat was hastily asked to check on the girls. It was after eight and she herself wanted an early night. She was not happy about this request but agreed. Angela made a few trustful friends, but they pretended to be only neighbours so as not to have

Francis, her controller, cause distress to her or to her friends.

Whilst Angela arranged for this impromptu babysitting Francis had gone down to prepare for the drive. He had explained that she should join him there. She left the block closing the huge metal door as quietly as possible so as not to disturb sleeping folk. The door squeaked sometimes. She saw him at the boot of the car but he was unable to see her since her footfalls went unheard over the soft grassed area. As she drew closer, she observed and heard the chink of metal as Francis took something out and shoved it into his right back pocket. When he saw her, he quickly closed the booth and climbed into the driver's seat. Angela got in and they moved off.

It was a fairly short drive to the dam, because after dark the usual families and tourists were absent. Parking was easy as there were only three to four cars in the car park therefore Francis had a choice of spaces and he elected to leave the Rover on the extreme right facing a wooded area. The roadway was at the rear but away also from the spotlights closer to the dam or on the entrance to a path into the woods. With the car safely parked he left and went to the booth again and spent a few minutes tinkering with tools or something.

Angela opened her passenger side door and placed one foot on the tarmac but when she tried to push the door farther open it would not give. Puzzled, she continued to try to force it to open so that she could put her other foot out but to no avail. The door felt as if it was held or pushed from outside, she could see no one or nothing which might prevent it from being opened. So, with a little more force she pushed harder to try to open that door. This time Angela became alarmed when at that final effort she heard what seemed to be a frantic cacophony of high-pitched voices raised in alarm as the door seemed to be pushed by some unseen force. She was perplexed. How should she explain what's happening to Francis It sounded weird to her anyway.

Francis by this time had leaned his head inside to ask Angela to hurry up. It's no good, she thought, she would not tell him the truth. Instead, she said to him that she had changed her mind, the voices ceased and she was able to return her left leg inside and pulled the door shut but kept a watchful eye to see if there were folk around playing a trick. But it held. Francis though was angry. 'Bl...y woman,' he exclaimed. She countered that it was her prerogative to change her mind and since she did not want to come, he should not be angry. A seething Francis fell silent, got into the car and drove off a lot more hastily than when he had arrived.

That incident had no specific explanation for her except that it may have been divine intervention again. As they arrived back in the families' quarters a furious Francis left the car and went to the booth again. He told her to go ahead and he would follow shortly. Angela had alighted and was part of the way across the grass when she reasoned that it would be silly to ring the door buzzer twice and disturb the residents within their block, so she walked back to wait for him to finish whatever he was doing in the booth. As she approached the car from the front, she had observed him remove something long and chunky enough for her to know that it was a large spanner from his back pocket and he had dropped it in the booth. Oh well, she mused, his daily job involved mechanics, so he was tinkering with the tools as he usually did.

However, it had then reminded her how he had tried to encourage her to fall into a frozen lake and that recollection made her try to work out these actions. They were all done furtively, that she saw, but why? The explanation which came into her mind was that during the daytime families went into that wooded area beside the dam. At night only couples ventured in, the path ran close to the edge of the dam which was cemented from the top down to the water in a sloping drop. An unfortunate foot slip on the left would be a sliding drop into the water below. He was aware that Angela could not swim – not that it would have made any difference since she would have been swallowed on contact into the churning water below. Why did he need a heavy spanner to take her presumably into that wood? The dam was well lit at night and there were guards on watch, therefore it had to have been a planned visit into that wood.   There was nowhere else to go.

Angela felt that this may be a wrong deduction, but he was predictable and she learned to be on alert. He was reluctant to spend any of his money on her at any time or to allow her too much housekeeping cash. It was always measured and checked by him in what he assumed to be a discreet manner but she chose to ignore this.

He was sent with his company to Unterjock - under the mountain - close to the Bavarian border on a training exercise to teach his men to ski. Angela knew where he was off to and did not expect him to return for two weeks. However, the odious woman visited her two days later to tell her that she needed to take the then two girls aged three and four to join Francis at the Pension Hotel in Unterjock for a short break. The train tickets were already purchased by the woman and her husband.

This was an utter surprise for Angela. He had organised her time to suit himself, to keep an eye on her with the excuse of a holiday break. She was anxious and alert, if it was above board any such message would have been through the usual official source, but he was being frugal as usual. The express train on the following day would take them to the terminus where Francis would be waiting with transport. That evening Angela had developed an alarming high temperature when Mrs Odious visited to check if she would be ready to leave for the train station at ten thirty in the morning. Observing the state that Angela was in, she went into action and summoned the doctor. Angela was aware of what was happening around her but was too ill to object. The woman took control.

She was given medication to lower her temperature and told that the doctor would check her again early in the morning. She did, but the fever remained high and she needed to be medicated still further as Angela's temperature had lowered only slightly. No way was Angela able to take control of her situation. Mrs Odious arrived soon after that doctor and did any packing that she felt was necessary before her husband arrived to take Angela and her children to the train station. A doped-up Angela and her two bewildered children were put on the train which stood at their ticketed platform and it pulled out five minutes before eleven in the morning. Their tickets she later noted, showed that they should have been on the eleven o'clock train but others made decisions and Angela, unable to make any, merely complied.

Unfortunately, that train they were put on was a stopping train and during the horrendous journey she and the children were shifted from seats to seats or needed to stand for a few stops. All the seats were reserved and the hostility to this foreign family continued to the terminus. On arrival Angela was so exhausted that she lacked the energy to find out whether they had arrived or not. Cheryl spied her father outside waiting and alerted her Mum. He needed to enter the carriage to assist her off.

It took her two days to recover from that fever - something which she had never had before and had not happened since, thank God. Was this a foreboding of something bad? The days passed by in a haze. The pension proprietor was openly hostile, but Francis never once supported or defended his wife. Each morning when their room was cleaned the duvet was stuck out of the window. It was the middle of winter - none of the other occupants got the same treatment. When ordering meals, they would look at Francis for confirmation before the order was made. One day he took them all out for a walk to the frozen river which divided Bavaria from Germany. Folk skied across back and forth daily, while at night the border guard with his large Alsatian hound visited the hotel for his usual beer and schnitzel. The children loved the dog and the guard gently coaxed them to stroke it.

On the way back from that frozen wasteland and river there was a hill or a high mound and Francis took the girls up and over himself because Angela had a phobia of falling and would not attempt the icy climb, the way down that iced-covered hill would be too steep for her also. She followed on the flat, on the right side until the ice beneath her feet begun to crackle. It felt unsafe, so she looked at Francis because he was familiar with the place so would know where she should walk. He stood at the top of the hill watching her. She indicated with open arms that she was not sure where to tread. He waved his arm for her to move even further to her right.

That did not seem valid therefore she carefully sidestepped to the left where the ice felt firmer. At that moment she looked ahead to see in the distance a young couple watching her dilemma and his odd indication which would take her into an iced-over lake or pond. He followed her gaze and hastily laughed using his hand to make a circling gesture that meant that Angela was mad. They never smiled or waved back but looked askance at him and eventually left but turned around two or three times to see the outcome. He was familiar with the lie of the land because it was part of his unit's training area. He used any opportunity to cause Angela distress, uncertainty and isolation so as to have control over her.

Chapter Seven
First Footing in Westphalia

Later in the year, on a cold dark December evening Francis took Angela for a First Footing experience. It sounded harmless so she agreed on that occasion for some unknown reason. She had learned not to accept some of his invitations at face value. He had led her into places which had alarmed her, with strangers who did not make her feel safe, on a few occasions he left her there, and she suspected that this was to be a compromising situation. Often, she had to talk her way out of what she suspected to be deliberately contrived schemes with other couples. Therefore, this was a surprise. Angela went along with this request to accompany him mainly because to decline the offer would antagonise him again also.

Francis lied about almost anything or presented his version to solicit compliance from her. She recalled this silly gaffe of his from their brief stay in Northern Ireland. As usual he lied about going with a mate one weekend to deep-sea fish. His mate had hired a boat. Okay, thought Angela, he needs time on his own anyway. Anyway, she asked: 'What would you like for supper because you said you would be late?' 'Oh, just beans on toast will do.' On his return from that "deep-sea" fishing trip Angela was presented with his prized catch - a trout!

Well, he was served his fried trout surrounded with baked beans. His expression was a treat to behold; a trout – he assumed that his alien wife was really dumb. She knew for sure that he went fishing however it was not for fish!

In one daytime incident when instead of Francis, another soldier arrived home at lunchtime he told her that her husband would be home later. Angela assumed he meant a few minutes later. The chap listened to her chatter over a cup of tea, then as he rose to leave, he remarked: 'You are too good for him you know; he does not deserve you.' Angela simply muttered thank you, unsure of whether those remarks were meant to be a compliment or an insult. It was a planned visit to send the chap to his place whilst he went to be with that man's wife. Angela had learned not to trust him, or even leave the children within his care. He grinned when his horrible odious friends belittled her with racist taunts which she was expected to receive as simply kidding. They were not.

This time of year, as expected and close to midnight, it was pretty dark and damp but to discover that they would be close to the woods or in what appeared to be a wooded area aroused Angela's suspicion. Earlier in their marriage she had found out how controlling Francis was. Someone who would talk to her in a calm voice but whose whole attitude could change in a split second, she was expected to agree with his comments, but Angela annoyed him with her own comments which angered him. He was dangerous, unpredictable and brutal. He had a penchant for throttling her if and whenever she became angry, but she had learned to remain calm during his threats and not allow him the satisfaction of seeing her fear.

They arrived in his car and after parking had made their way under a green, black sky to a row of houses which appeared to be overhung with large trees. A middle-aged man emerged from the gloom on to a narrow roadway or it may have been a path. He greeted them before turning to greet others as they emerged in the semi-light. If there were streetlights she was unable to see them. This man seemed to be assertive and Angela guessed that he may be their leader/organiser from the manner in which others addressed him and waited for instructions. He looked her up and down and made a comment in German that solicited a burst of laughter from the group. Angela became uncomfortable but Francis as usual joined in this discomforting gesture although his German was negligible. It was his normal behaviour towards his wife to humiliate her publicly or to apologise for her ignorance.

She had no idea where they were, nor did Francis bother to disclose any such details therefore she was dependent on his goodwill amongst strangers in that strange area. It would not have been the first time that Angela was placed in a situation when she was forced to make a decision to walk back to their flat alone. The car drive though, from the family quarters had been relatively short, though there were too many turns to recognise or to recall. Was it her lack of suitable apparel which solicited that mirth? She could not say. As people gathered around, she noted that all wore thick winter clothing, men in lederhosen - leather trousers, hats or berets on which some had added an adornment of a feather, as well as holding walking sticks. All carried rucksacks on their backs. The women though fewer, also were attired warmly in pants and walking boots, and had the standard rucksack.

Before setting off as per instructed by the leader, Angela was offered a drink of something which the gruff leader had poured from a flask pulled out from within his rucksack. She looked askance at Francis for help because she was a newcomer to alcohol. Francis, who stood closer to the group away from Angela and did not seem to want her near to him, merely looked at her and indicated with his hand that she swallowed the contents in one gulp. Not wanting to annoy him and others who watched she did swallow the aniseed scented but throat-burn liquid. In the semi-darkness another younger man from the first house came out to lean against his doorpost to stand with folded arms and watch her. His gaze was intent, and no way would Angela allow him the satisfaction to see her chicken out of this challenge. Well, that was the thought anyway.

Oh dear! That drink took effect within seconds, her eyes went funny, and unable to see clearly, she stumbled and knew that her legs had buckled and that she would fall. However, out of the corner of her eye she saw the observer as he strode towards her and with his pair of strong arms lifted and carried her indoors, to a settee. She may have protested but everything had become hazy she had no idea how long she was out. To her chagrin, she opened fog-filled eyes and saw the strong-armed chap sat in a rocking chair, or it might have been a large chair - intently studying her. It was very discomforting and embarrassing. She felt as if it was a wake with her as the cadaver on the gurney – the settee – and the sole observer keeping wake.

Angela sat up and returned a brief stare that made him quickly rise from his seat as if he had been sprung. He rushed off and entered a kitchen, she had assumed, to speak with a woman. Angela had a brief glimpse of the back of a woman in a floral dress and an apron perhaps. That person spoke to him in a chiding voice and he returned to offer a glass of water. Then with a bowl of something crunchy to eat he had promptly occupied his scrutiny seat to observe once more. There was no hostility from him just curiosity perhaps. It was much later when she learned that German students learn French and English at school.

Once Angela had become aware of her surroundings out of whatever stupor that had almost felled her, she swung her legs off the settee and sat to contemplate her dilemma. It left her seething at Francis and anxious about the children back indoors. Questions churned in her mind, she was unsure about communicating with her hosts in their language and simply sat quietly to contemplate what to do. She feared that Francis had really carried out his threat and had dumped her. She had no idea where, nor how to return to care for her children. She would not have minded if he had done this in a city or at least a familiar area, but here, where was she? He had repeatedly told her that she should go – to leave the children because they were his, and that she should not become too fond of them. That had caused her to emotionally distance herself from her children, but instinct warned her that she needed to care for them until they were older.

Eventually, Francis turned up and entered the home as if he was familiar with the folk there and her fears turned to relief. She rose and thanked her hosts for looking after her then followed Francis to the car park. As Angela turned from thanking her unwitting hosts, Francis resorted to his base instinct and had remarked quietly to her: 'Oh, he is only a young guy.' It became clear that he was expecting his wife to engage in a fantasy as he himself would have done.

It seemed like a long time before Francis returned to collect her to return to their two toddlers. She did note that if was an event where alcohol was drunk, he should be bleary-eyed as was his norm but he appeared to be sober. Anyway, he had to drive so that maybe limited his intake of spirits. She never made any comments about his behaviour but knew instinctively that in future she must be on her guard. Francis tried to engage her in conversation but Angela tactfully feigned ignorance, it was safer. Once again, she was manoeuvred by her husband into an awkward situation, and felt embarrassed and humiliated. Was this situation contrived or was it accidental? The offered alcoholic drink seemed to have been a deliberate ploy to learn whether she was to be included on the walk or not. It seemed not, since she was left behind to wait for her husband's probable return.

Angela felt helpless because of the young children in her care, she knew what it felt like as a child to be left with strangers, some of whom had not been pleased and had ill-treated herself and her sister. Her own childhood experiences kept her going regardless. It was her focus on that unhappy marriage. Their father made it clear that he was finished with her after the Army moved out of Northern Ireland. What Francis said and what he did then had confused her. Ten years after they were married and had separated Angela quizzed their best man. Mitch would be sent by his concerned wife to bring the three much needed food supplies, and instructions to bring them down to Buckinghamshire for hot baths.

At that time, their gas was cut off because benefits were being processed and the gas bill was not settled. On a visit to their bank for money - which was a joint account but used by Angela only to withdraw her housekeeping cash - on Francis's instructions. Angela had a nasty racist insult from a well-known national British bank. The manager told her that the joint account was closed and there were no funds available, but that he may be able to help her. He would give her money so that she could return to her native country. Angela, unaware of his implication replied sorry but she would not be allowed to take the children out of the UK. 'Oh, they would not have to go with you, they would go into care' he corrected. She was speechless. As she pondered his offensive remark she realised that he may have been a member of that racist xenophobic political party. She left a little wiser about this kind of hatred.

Why had Francis married her? He would tell her to go but if she attempted to do so, her passport and personal belongings from her mother and sister were hidden. Their best man had then explained, somewhat reluctantly, after observing her distress, he did not want to hurt Angela's feelings but that Francis had a dilemma on his hands in Northern Ireland. He had gladly agreed that posting to Guyana because he was fearful of the family of the Irish girl whom he had made pregnant and had told her that he would wed her. She was awaiting his return to marry her. It was a relief to learn this truth. He had told so many lies to different people and had spun a web from which it would be impossible to extricate himself.

Chapter Eight
The Fantasist

Just months after being married she observed him as he indulged in his fantasies. In bed she would be asked if she ever considered being with film stars. Directing a puzzled look and a negative reply at him, he would begin to fantasise in explicit detail. That behaviour seemed a trifle weird and at times she thought that maybe it was her, that she must be the odd one. Not so, it was all in his head Angela later learned, although he would try to make it happen. She noted how he would cover his tracks with lies to get out of situations. He boasted about 'the son' he had left in Germany. When a curious Angela asked whether he sent money for the child's upkeep he had replied with an air of dismissal: 'Oh, the mother doesn't want any money. She told me so.' Years of experience with him made her aware that that was not true.

Angela did wonder how he had convinced that girl in Northern Ireland that he could not marry or accommodate her in his life. He had probably used Angela as his alibi. The girl though, was openly hostile to Angela whom she attempted to push around when they met in the washroom at a mess social. Angela never got angry though. It became the norm for her to see young women drink and socialise without any inhibitions. No, she thought the behaviour of the girl on that evening was due to too much imbibing. Anyway, that incident was cut short by the timely intervention of a few of the other wives who were more acquainted with this situation and of Francis's reputation, from their husbands.

A few weeks later the girl spotted the lone pregnant Angela in an isolated bus terminal. Angela watched as the girl, then sober and with a child on her hip, deliberately strode across the road to fire quick bursts of questions: 'Do you love him? Is this your first child?' Angela answered calmly not sure of what to make of it. Meanwhile her friend remained across the road shouting: 'Leave her alone, she does not know anything.' She eventually turned with a look of disbelief to join her friend and left Angela alone once more. It was tiring to stand and wait for a bus in that isolated place, so it was a relief to see the bus arrive. Her legs also were numb from standing for several minutes.

Whew! That was a relief she thought on hearing their best man with the truth. Until that moment Angela had harboured feelings of guilt and personal recriminations that it was her selfish desires which got her into hot water, and how she felt compelled to endure his behaviour. However, this revelation that they had both used each other was a relief. He was a coward, who went to great lengths to present to observers a strong united marriage.

The six-foot two, thirteen stone Francis used brawn to exert control to fulfil his desire for respectability. Whatever grey matter was left upstairs was used to plot his seedy goals and to satiate his lust. Most of it was fantasy of course. He would use people mostly unsuspecting women and then disappear. Any female was a potential to him, if not at first sight then he would return at a convenient time when they were alone. Some of his gains however were from bored, desperate women. Now he had a wife to use as his excuse to cover his irresponsible errant behaviour. These were not affairs - that meant nothing to him, and he was apprehensive of any of those women making claims on him it was – as he would remark; just one of those things.

She knew that he would eventually leave, his erratic behaviour, his charade of being respectable amongst folk, especially before senior ranks. His oafishness had earned him open disgust and the debasing of his wife to impress others. His bravado and perceived helplessness were there to impress his family. Most of all Angela learned not to ask him for money for clothes or anything for herself. His reply would be maybe next month, as there were not enough funds in the bank at that time. There never were.

He was self-centred in everything, even his own children got sweets to keep them happy and little else. Angela was informed that it was none of her business how much he earned in the army. He retained all bank statements and other legal documents in a locked briefcase stored in his car. However, when his wife received letters from her family or any monies from part-time employment, he made it his duty to read everything.

She had her first and only experience of First Footing, the tradition she later learned of greeting the New Year in and seeing the old year out. It meant walking along knocking on doors, having a chat and sharing a glass of schnapps and a slice of cured sausage. Oh well never mind, Angela mused, she would survive to relate it all with amusement.

Following that December escapade, life with Francis returned to his normal bolshie behaviour –"me Tarzan, you Jane". She was always wary when he behaved nicely to her. How many soldiers went on three-week exercises and returned with the smell of a hospital on them? His guilt was obvious. She would be presented with a small bunch of flowers from a sheepish Francis. Angela allowed him to believe that he was clever. When he had been offered a promotion, it had caused him to tremble at the prospect of responsibility. Curious!

It would take many years later before Angela understood that Francis's desire was for respectability not responsibility. He went out of his way on many occasions to accommodate requests for help from other wives - or so he once explained to his wife - at the behest of his own family or his meals.   Often, she would be sniggered at by other wives when they were out shopping in the NAAFI. Little did they know that she would have happily donated him to their butcher's block.

It may have been weeks or months that lapsed following that December evening, when Francis arrived home for lunch one day. He held a small but very pretty black wrought iron table. It had fluted legs, two pale blue and two peach tiles diagonally aligned. He handed it to Angela with the words –'he made it, said it was for you'. Oh, she wondered who "he" was. Francis said it was that bloke she was with. He had a way of saying things that sounded more like an accusation. This was news to Angela. She needed to ask forthright questions, but past experience taught her to be cautious and not to seem overtly interested.

Actually, she had a sneaking feeling that he had acquired it somehow. He never gave her anything of value and destroyed or lost her valued possessions.   Therefore, her initial thought was - oh God, what has he done now?

No, this came from the chap who had rescued her that evening – the one who leant on the side of that house on that gloomy night. Francis said that he made it himself, it was his hobby. Relief, it was quite pretty, and she accepted it as cautiously as she dared. Do not make a fuss or Francis will destroy it, she told herself. Anyway, what puzzled her was how had the chap managed to persuade him to deliver it intact.

Chapter Nine
Sudden change of heart

Their shaky marriage continued until Francis became fed up with the Army. He wanted out but had not completed the required sign-up period. So, he asked Angela if she would like to see her relatives who resided in Canada. What? Of course, she agreed, but suspected it was just a bait to let her down again. No, it was a bait all right but directed at the Army as his reason for leaving – his wife wanted to see her family. From then until they left for the UK, he would use this excuse. It was Angela who wanted him to leave. He would never disclose to her his true reason though. She was not his confidante. Her role was to encourage him in whatever decisions he made. Question was though what had he done to urge him to make such a decision? He had been behaving oddly for a few weeks, very quiet and unusually attentive to his family. Now he wanted to run, but why?

Angela knew that he wanted to feel in control. His job in the Army required an expectation to obey orders, not to question or argue. His marriage offered him the opportunity to assert his control. His wife would be at his mercy, never allowed to entertain any notions of feeling his equal, even though at times he relied on her opinions. Any decisions would be expressed as his own. Right at the onset of their married life he had made it clear that her desire to prepare herself in any formal training for work was out of the question. After attending to their first born, Angela left the room leaving the door slightly ajar. As the front room door was quietly closed behind her, she overheard him angrily say – 'I don't want you to feel that you are better than me'. Angela's initial thought was that he was very insecure. Time would lead her to learn that it was not insecurity just plain spitefulness. He wanted to exert control to be his inferior. Her personal needs would be at his discretion.

However, it may have been that the Army was fed up with him. They had hoped that once he was married and had a family, that such responsibility would be his anchor and that his bullish, racist behaviour would improve. Francis though had other plans or perhaps was urged to make decisions even though they may have been unacceptable to regimental protocol. He had recommended an unsavoury man for promotion which allowed the couple subsequent use of the Sergeants' Mess's only facilities and privileges. Francis had in effect compromised the reputation of that Mess and chose to ignore this.

The Army shunned the couple because of their notorious behaviour and subsequent reputation. Francis ignored any rebuffs and did his utmost to include them in whatever event emerged. Perhaps the man had some sort of a hold on him because no matter how much others loathed and ignored them Francis always included them in his social and work-related life, even to keeping an eye on his wife. This man may have been acquainted with Francis during his demotion. Usually however, soldiers seldom socialise outside their rank. Therefore, whatever activity Francis and this man were involved in would have to be curtailed or the man was able to be raised to Francis's rank for their association to continue. Which would explain why Francis was adamant to propose the promotion for that individual despite disapproval from others.

Something which had nagged at Angela- was back when he had returned home from work one afternoon and she had observed him literally shaking. His explanation that he had been offered a promotion but was not sure that he would be able to handle 'it' sounded lame. That to Angela seemed a curious reaction. He had been demoted in the past because of his attitude and behaviour then promoted after marriage. That unusual reaction set Angela thinking.

It was prior to that supposed offer of promotion, after he and his sidekick mate returned from an assumed reconnoitre exercise in Canada – or so he had informed Angela. When she had quizzed him about what state and where they were stationed, he responded with vague answers. He could not remember the state or area and did not do much sightseeing either. Did he and his mate really go to Canada? She recalled how he had reacted when she had reminded him to take his passport. His vague reply had been: 'Oh yes, I would need that, wouldn't I'?

Shortly after he had returned, she had noticed how pensive he had become, even his usual bullishness abated to a lesser degree, and also there was that profound medical odour on him. Angela welcomed this respite but watched and listened to his vague replies. It would be a few weeks later when he suggested emigrating to Canada, using her as his reason of course to leave the forces. Why then? She suspected that he had done something not kosher, and it had caused him to become unsettled. He had known nothing but army life for many years. He tolerated the discipline because being under the protection of HM Forces, he felt confident of protection in any event of trouble.

Therefore, it was a surprise to observe a new but cautious enthusiasm entering his thinking. What had he done? Was it something which would have brought disgrace to the regiment, possibly due to the actions of a senior rank as he was? This seemed to be a pattern with him. When he was up against situations beyond his control, he reasoned that it was time to flee or hide. Whatever dubious activity he had been engaged in had triggered a kind of fear in him anyway and it seemed more as if this or apprehension was this driving force. Angela went along with his suggestion to go to Canada. If that happened, then she would be closer to her family.

Also, married life curbed his seamy dubious activities encouraged of course by his mate and wife. Angela hated mess socials because she was told to sit with the odious pair and to socialise. They chain-smoked, made crude jokes, jibed at her reluctance to join in and also at Francis for "not being able to control his wife". 'She's got you under her thumb, Francis'. When Angela was invited into conversation with folk from other tables, the woman would shout 'Oy, you are with us'.

Angela loved music and dancing. It was how she passed her teenage years with friends but on the few occasions to dance he ended up being an embarrassment. His dance moves were unique to observe. He looked like Dumbo struggling for take-off or to be more exact, like a constipated turkey, and the other folk on the floor gave him a wide berth. Angela turned her back and did her bit but felt silly dancing on her own. He grinned stupidly at his antics, well at least he enjoyed himself, but Angela didn't nor did others. She was deterred from socialising with anyone, and if she seemed too chummy with others, he would appear to remind her to circulate or say something crass at which folk would turn away. Others were bold enough to ask her outright: 'Why did you marry him'? He was so thick skinned that he merely grinned and moved her away.

Chapter Ten
No more Army life

He was given a lump sum on his early voluntary retirement since he was almost at the end of his tenure. He had cash in his pocket and a blank canvas to restart life outside of orders. He had informed her that he had made application for them to emigrate to Canada. It never happened. Angela was excluded from the final interview at the Canadian Embassy. As usual, he told her to sit in the waiting area with the children. An hour later, an emergent Francis looked thunderous, so she asked no questions then. Later he disclosed that they would not be going to live in Canada, no reason given to her, nor did she ask why.

He had probably failed the medical or been refused because of his past record, she had assumed. Over the years she learned from other sources about Francis's ebullient behaviour, his demotions from Sergeant to Private and his unacceptably racist attitude towards the lower ranks. He had form. The army tried to instil a sense of responsibility and respectability, but alas to no avail. In his teenage years he had been part of a motorbike gang the members of which prided themselves on being real blue suede shoes guys, the popular guys and perhaps this gang culture attitude remained with him. One such boast was that Cliff Richard, Harry Webb is his real name, as Francis repeatedly reminded her, was part of their club. Francis boasted about his ego by continually demeaning others and therefore Angela was never impressed.

So, what now Angela mulled. Aware that they had no place to live and the money in his pocket was quickly being used on trivial purchases, such as sweets, cigarettes, petrol, etc, she needed to do something or the children would be left with his family while he would then surmise that she was no longer needed. Angela had an opportunity to discuss the dilemma at his sister's home. He had arrived with his family, without prior invitation or consideration for his sister's plans, as was the norm.

However, in her presence he would be unable or unwilling to shush Angela. His sister suggested to them to consider purchasing property as a secure base. Throughout this discussion he tried to apologise about lack of funds, not sure which area he wanted to live in and so on. Anyway, it was an opportunity that he would not be able to back out of without his sister understanding that he was not committed to providing for his family.

Visits to estate agents became a hurdle she had to overcome as she observed how he carefully selected the most awful properties to view. She became wise to this crafty ruse and on their next visit to an agent she boldly walked inside to enquire of possible affordable properties in better areas. The manager of one responded to her query and produced details of a suitable four bed semi-detached in a popular area, whose details would be on public display later. It was a snip, but it required a little work on the roof. That was how they managed to secure a home. That roof job was never done two years later when the house was sold. In fact, very little was done indoors or out as Francis really had no interest in domestic affairs. Once he had signed the documents he felt empowered to do as he wished. He possessed property which meant money for him; it was a boost to his morale that lasted at least for nine months.

To rid himself of boredom he continually picked arguments with Angela and hit out when she ignored him. He taunted her with remarks that she needed to see a psychiatrist. She became tired and worn down with his mental abuse and she did in fact make an appointment to speak to a psychiatrist. The day of her appointment arrived, and she set off early to keep the one o'clock date. So engrossed was she with thoughts of what to say that she walked past the building and went to sit in the waiting room of a building further up where the door was wide open. With two minutes to spare someone appeared to enquire how they could assist. She started to tell the woman about her appointment with the psychiatrist but was stopped with; 'oh my dear you are in the waiting room of the STD treatment clinic'. 'What is that?' she asked. Learning what it meant, she promptly exploded with laughter.

That was hilarious, a laughing apology was made as she scurried off to retrace her steps so as not to keep the psychiatrist waiting. Still laughing at her gaffe, the man offered her a seat and listened through Angela's mirth for about ten minutes. He then stopped her and said: 'If you are able to laugh at yourself as you are doing then in my opinion there is nothing wrong with your mental health. However,' he continued, 'from what you said I saw that your marriage is causing you problems. Sort that out and you will be okay.' She was not mad after all. Angela left relieved but a trifle disappointed at not being able to solve her dilemma at home.

Very soon the idea of him settling down began to bore him; the jobs offered bored him; spending his money on house and family bored him. Angela found herself forced to be a partner to his light-fingeredness. Why pay when he could get it free, was his mantra. Angela managed to ignore or overlook his crass stupidity for appearing home with floral orange curtains, green felt floor tiles, a workbench and tools which he had no idea how to use and other odds and ends.

She once tentatively raised her concerns to a retired policeman who advised her not to say anything as she would be liable for aiding and abetting. Great to know! Bullied at home and bullied by the law, so she shrugged her shoulders in resignation. There was a great deal to learn, once they had settled into civilian life. Her children were accepted she saw, but she was not. Most of the curiosity was folk being nosy and a reluctance to accept her.

Francis became more restless and his aggression increased. There was no one to stop him from being a racist, controlling bully apart from reporting incidents to the police. This was tedious because they wanted to know if there were bruises or witnesses. He had punched Angela directed towards her heart one day, again when she had disagreed on something. It was delivered with the force and intensity of a boxer. As she bounced off the fireplace and regained her breath, she looked him in the eye and asked: 'Did that make you feel like a man? Then, better look into a mirror, because all I can see is a wild animal.' He had the temerity to appear contrite and to apologise but she simply scorned him. He was a shallow and weak individual, a mere bully throwing his weight about.

After they had settled in a home of their own she secretly acquired a mail order catalogue for birthdays and Christmas things for the children, a portable sewing machine so that she'd be able to make clothes for them instead of making them up hand sewn, and a vacuum cleaner to replace a hand brush and dustpan. He was seriously mean, but Angela would not allow the children to go without. When he saw her determination to get what was needed he made promises to help pay for purchases which were paid for out of child allowance (which was paid to the mother then) and he would refund her at the end of the month. That never happened either.

He had an account with an exclusive men's clothing shop and often kitted himself out with new clothes including socks. They were costly because he bought cashmere, linen and cotton and he knew they were what respectable gents wore. 'Mutton dressed as lamb' Angela learned was the expression used by folk such as Francis. What amazed her was his lack of appreciation for his extravagances. He wore a newly bought beautiful soft grey cashmere sweater it to paint the garage door with orange paint (pilfered from somewhere) whilst standing on the little table which was a gift to Angela, and duly splashed paint on both. The sweater was dumped, considered ruined. Angela shopped in charity shops or made clothes for herself and the girls from secret purchases of "surprise bundles of fabric"..

In another disagreement, she was grabbed by the neck and forced against the window - to show her how easy it would be to rape her. Unfortunately, as usual he had misjudged her ability to retaliate. On the windowsill behind her stood a three-inch-high heavy brass ornament from his mother's church which was gifted to her and later given to him. With her left-hand Angela picked it up and whacked him square on his forehead. It broke the skin and he had stepped back, stunned that she had wounded him when he saw blood trickle down.

Angela became aware that he was intent on swift retaliation therefore she pushed past him and ran out of the house. He pursued her but managed to trip her as she was almost in the telephone booth. A passing motorist witnessed this, but he quickly behaved as if it was a practical joke. This was to prevent her reporting his behaviour. He eventually calmed down at home and she warned him again that if he continued to physically abuse her or the children, she would report him to the police. If that ornament was on the right-side things may have been worse, because she was right-handed. That incident with the brass ornament may have momentarily stopped an alarming situation but it made her feel very scared of how she may be forced to protect herself.

She had reported his behaviour twice before, but as usual no charges were made. Only warnings were issued to him which he ignored, of course. Once after he taunted her that she could not leave or bring charges, because he owned the house and that the children would not be allowed to go with her, she had left without her personal items. She reported him and the police accompanied her to collect her things. None of these could be found. He had hidden them all. It would be months later when the second daughter had revealed where he had hidden things having been sworn to secrecy.

After he returned from work, Angela was normally told to get on with meal preparations. His reasoned excuse was that he did not have much opportunity to be with his children. One day she heard a whimper and looked through to the living room to see him slapping the eldest about her head whilst ordering her to stop crying. Angela was incensed and knowing that he would flatten her if she physically intervened, she called out a stupid remark instead to hopefully stop him. 'That's right, knock her brains out. That will surely stop her crying.' It worked. He stopped mid-hand from his next slap, to direct a baleful look at Angela. Not to be outmanoeuvred by Angela's interference, he followed their daughter as she fled in tears up to her room to warn and to threaten her with false fatherly care advice.

No explanation why he struck her was given to Angela, not from the twelve-year-old who had been hit or from her eleven-year-old sister who appeared to be guilty and avoided looking directly at her mother. The youngest simply cringed with fear and alarm that she may be next, so she tried to make herself appear inconspicuous on the settee by covering herself with cushions.

As Angela was not encouraged to be part of family times, she was unaware of his devious strategy to divide the children. The middle one he had apparently told when she was about three or four- was to be his love, his favourite. She looked a bit like him. Even Angela was not allowed to discipline her and that had caused major problems and resentment as that child used to take advantage of the other two in any way that she could. She and Cheryl were always at loggerheads over something or other, and when Angela tried to encourage them to sort out their differences Cheryl would accuse her mother of not being impartial. Denise created her problems but always wailed when she felt aggrieved. When they retaliated at her overtly disruptive behaviour, she would complain to her Dad who ordered them to behave nicely towards their sister. That division continues to this day.

Angela was to learn how deep this division had become when the couple had sat before a judge to settle contributions and so on. Francis, as usual, tried to take control and be clever and told the judge that he was willing to consider maintenance for the middle child only, because he knew that he had sired her. However, as he was away on exercises most of his army days, he did not know who the father of the other two were. That poor judge's expression! It was one of pure incredulity. He was gobsmacked.

In civilian life they rarely socialised. Babysitters were very difficult to find and this was the drawback for Francis. There had been endless lower ranks to draw on for babysitting, when they were part of the army, but that was now lost to him. He knew no other male friends close enough to 'visit the local for a drink' either. He liked whisky, it made him feel power-driven and imbibing indoors, though tiresome, appeared to revive the Cheshire cat inane expression on him. Sleeping off its effects posed no problem. He could sleep on a bed of snow which made him whiter than white but a hot bath soon revived him.

She was being pushed to do something awful. One day she may go further and really hurt him and this scared her. He stood close to her one day blowing cigarette smoke into her face. The intention was to provoke an argument and then physically abuse her. She had been doing his laundry in the kitchen sink, because he would not allow her to buy a washing machine but kept promising. That was his usual reason for them not having things – cannot afford it as yet maybe later. Later never arrived.

Angela tried to tolerate the provocation until anger got the better of her and she emptied the freshly made pot of tea over him. It scalded him from neck to waist down on his right side. She contemplated using the pot also, but that would be needed. He swore loudly, but she wasn't in a mood to be sympathetic. He was in pain and angry but she ignored his yelps and ran out of the house for fresh air to calm down. He followed of course but she hid somewhere along the main road and watched him drive past several times searching for her. She spent that evening at the nursing home where she was employed. She did not have any intention to kill him but to maim him in some way perhaps. However, that would not be a good solution because it would mean her having to care for him for the remainder of his or her life and she did not want that.

There was an alarming incident where she felt that was a grave warning for her safety. They retired to bed one evening and Angela went into a deep sleep. She suddenly awoke to see him stood against his side of the bed in a frightening posture. Truly, he had looked like a picture of a

Neanderthal with an animal or apelike posture. Both his arms were down by his sides and she had noted how his fingers were spread in a grab position. However, it was the eyes which caught her immediate attention. They were the most frightening things to see – he had one green and one grey eye normally - this time they were dilating uncontrollably.

With her innate instinct she knew it would be unwise if she showed any sign of fear or reacted in alarm. So, she feigned tiredness and said: 'Can't you sleep? Come to bed, it is getting cold.' She patted his side of the bed. Then she immediately turned her back to whatever was stood glaring at her. Perhaps too, it was her time to observe him in his true character of a Neanderthal. He definitely behaved like one of those humanoids.

If it was to attack, then so be it. There would be no point in being fearful. Sleep had gone from her completely and she waited for him to respond or to carry out whatever he intended. It seemed a long time before she heard and felt him lie with his back to her and she knew that he was not asleep. In fact, he did not sleep for the remainder of that night. He simply lay rigid feigning sleep. He was definitely in the grip of some uncontrollable force because it took him a long time to emerge from it and to respond to her request. That had definitely alarmed her, and she had to do something soon. That primitive expression had also been noted before when he had punched her in her chest.

No, there must be a way of putting an end to their situation. He definitely would not divorce her. That would not please his Catholic family, even though he had no respect for religion or God. Therefore, she had to find a way out somehow. She also had become anxious of him infecting her due to his seamy lifestyle. Thankfully, one helpful action she had taken was to sign them under one general practitioner at their health clinic. In the Forces army personnel were treated by a different doctor from that of the families. That new GP had access to both their records now and was aware of things that could affect Angela's health. He had warned Francis to leave or that he would be forced to submit evidence against him if necessary. That had enraged Francis, but he was intent to cause as much disruption to her and the children's lives before going. That GP's sympathetic treatment allowed her to feel a little more certain that she needed to take care of her own health, so that she would be able to provide the care that the children needed.

Angela visited the city one day while the children were at school and Francis was at work. On her way home she mulled over her and the children's situation. Either she went or he went, but he would not have allowed her to decide. If the situation turned angry and she voiced her concern he became annoyed, aggressive and physically abused her. Even the children were wary of him. Well at least the eldest and youngest were.

Chapter Eleven
Divorce

As her footsteps brought her to notice an overhead sign for solicitors - she hesitated. Okay, she thought, here goes nothing and went inside to an empty waiting area. With no one in sight she turned to leave when a door opened, and a man approached to speak to her. A few minutes later she was ushered into the presence of a ginger-haired female lawyer. A moment of uncertainty made her hesitate. The person appeared quite stern. Oh dear, thought Angela, would she be dismissed, or would this person agree to offer her some kind of assistance? Yes, the woman would listen. At last, someone to talk to. She felt relieved and as anyone in the midst of a confusing situation knew, she tried to explain. She sounded jumbled and confused, unbelievable to her own ears. Angela was asked to go away, write down her problems and possible solution then return. This she eagerly did though in secret.

On her follow-up visit she was pleased that this lawyer would help. The divorce papers which Angela was asked to present for Francis's signature and agreement were eventually passed to him. It took a bit of courage to do that. Francis merely sniggered and said she was a woman, a foreigner and in more derogatory racist terms, she would not be allowed to leave unless he allowed and he would not do so. She knew how he would react, and the lawyer had advised her to be patient. He would sign.

He did, hoping that it would be thrown out by a judge. It was accepted to proceed, and this alarmed Francis so he changed tactics and did the usual trick of pleading stupidity, apologising and promising to change. She considered this for a while. Was she depriving the girls of a father? Anyway, she reasoned he was not particularly concerned about their welfare or he would have considered either leaving to allow them to be cared by Angela or demonstrate that love he professed to have for his children- when it suited him. She conceded. After learning that she had cancelled the procedure he laughed and told her he would not allow her to leave until he was ready.

Needless to say, her lawyer was not pleased when she approached her three months later. However, there could be a loophole, the lawyer told her. Francis had not cancelled his petition, he had never felt that he needed to do so, and that error on his part allowed the stalled proceedings to be resumed. He grew angrier and more nasty tempered. Even the children became more anxious, unsettled and argued about everything and nothing in particular. They also felt defenceless when he displayed his manpower to them or to their mother. They found it difficult to relax when he was around but tried to appear settled. It may be true to say that it was never a united family unit. His wife and children were his possessions to do as he wished for or with them.

His legal representatives sent copious letters of complaints and threats demanded by Francis of course. One such was to order Angela to take the middle child back into the family home. She wanted to live with him, after he made promises to her which he could not nor not ever keep. Social Services whom he had asked to, "keep an eye on Angela in his concern for his children," were alerted to check on the child in his care. They compiled a report which deemed him unsuitable as a parent and issued an order for him to return her home. Whatever he told the child caused her to become aggressive and destructive towards Angela.

Isolation and mental control. That was what he practised continuously to force her to depend completely on him. His targets included: acquaintances, other wives whilst in the Army, friends, teachers or anyone with whom Angela became too friendly. On visits to his own family, she was primed before they had set out from home - to amuse herself with walks in their garden or whatever, until he had had a moment to talk with his family. Then she could enter and be allowed in on any conversation. They were not Angela's family he would constantly remind her; they were his alone and Angela should not ever feel that she was welcome. It was his way to subdue her and perhaps she would eventually become worn down.

Even though they were officially separated, he continued to disrupt their lives. The children decided to sleep together in the adjoining bedroom for warmth and security. Early one morning, around four thirty, the eldest woke Angela. She was scared because she had heard someone climbing the drainpipe outside the adjoining bathroom. Angela went into the bathroom to investigate and saw Francis balanced halfway up the pipe trying to reach the window. He had the chutzpah to ask her to open the window for him to enter. She closed the curtains, applied the window lock and told the children to return to bed and to ignore him. His explanation later was that he had come for access to his children.

Another incident which should have taught him a lesson was on an access visit late in the day when he asked to sleep in the spare room because it was a long drive back to Sussex. The girls pleaded for him to stay the night. Angela was reluctant to disappoint them or deprive them of his company. During the night however, she heard scratching sounds outside her bedroom, and him telling one of the girls who also left their room to investigate, to return to bed as everything was okay. He had armed himself with a couple of tools and sat scraping wood around the hinges on her bedroom door – to remove the door because Angela had locked it. Angela was not alarmed. It was her stupid husband, so she waited with some amusement for the outcome.

He managed to remove the bedroom door and entered to declare that he had come for his conjugal rights as they were not yet a divorced couple. She never said a word as he stepped backwards against the double wardrobe immediately to his rear to gain momentum to perform a running leap on to the bed. As she watched the performance, the wardrobe fell on top of him and he was flattened face down towards the foot of the bed. He began to yell begging her to help him out. Angela rose casually and left the bedroom. She had decided to allow him privacy to become more intimate with his wardrobe. His favourite child saw his predicament and said to her mother: 'Mum, we need to help Dad to get out or he'll get hurt.' 'Oh no,' Angela replied, 'he is big and strong and will get out on his own. Leave him.' The wardrobe had become unstable because it stood on one of the floorboards which he had prised open further along to hide all Angela's personal items. Yes, revenge had been exacted and Angela enjoyed the spectacle. She found him watching TV early in the morning before he left.

It was all sorted in the end, the decree nisi coming late in 1980 followed by the absolute. With a sigh of relief Angela felt ready but apprehensive at the probability of restoring a form of stability for the children. The council moved the family to a populated village with a mix of council estate and other houses. Francis went to the trouble to find out where they had moved to, from the removal firm, using the pretence of forgetting the new address. Then his car would appear at the schools, in front of their new home and waiting until he was ready to leave. Still, he continued to seethe at Angela's chutzpah to outmanoeuvre him. Angela needed to be home to walk the children to and from school. They felt as though they were being stalked and that created tension, anxiety and stress for them all. Added to that was a couple of yobs; lager louts as the police had referred to them. They tormented the girls after school. Angela needed to be present to protect them from the daily annoyance.

One final spiteful act Francis dealt on Angela was to place a burden on the eldest child of thirteen telling her to keep an eye on her mother because she was not well. After noting Cheryl's constant concern and enquiry about 'how are you feeling, Mum?' Angela reassured her daughter that she should ignore that instruction as it was only his spitefulness. It was a relief when she relaxed to pursue her own interests.

It was also a relief when Angela learned that Francis had emigrated to the USA with his share from the sale of their home. He was in effect an illegal immigrant there and was anxious to find a way to remain. Apparently, he had informed his solicitor that his sister in the USA had sent for him therefore his solution was to wed a single parent. He ran out on her when she decided to have IVF and gave birth to triplets. He needed a base cover not more responsibility. Was she aware that Francis had had a vasectomy? Anyway, he soon latched himself on to another single parent with a grown child and quickly married her. He then spent a few years with this third wife before dying of lung cancer. Thank goodness someone else had that burden. Nor were his lawyers ever paid for services during the divorce. Nice chap Francis! Angela came into possession of a slip of paper with this healthy advice:

Sin will take you further than you wanted to go;

Keep you there longer than you wanted to stay;

Cost you more than you are willing to pay.

Alas, some folk never want to acknowledge this possibly because it is too great a challenge for them to deal with.

Those women had to be independent or with grown children because he would disappear again in any demand for financial support. This was why he fled his second wife. She met his errant middle child and decided that she wanted to have children with him. She hoped that he would fund her fertility treatment. When three babies arrived at once he disappeared. Angela learned this from Denise who was urged by the woman to ask for Angela's assistance in claiming maintenance for her three babies. The woman's church also sent requests for details about Francis himself. Of course, Angela refused to comply on the grounds that she had fought for her own freedom without help so why should she interfere? That woman was in her native land with access to legal and other resources that Angela had not had.

All that Angela wanted to be sure of was that he would not be returning to harass her or their children. As far as she was concerned he could go off to Timbuktu and get lost. He would not be missed. Sweet revenge was hers when he was forced to exile himself from his home and family. It was his own downfall, orchestrated by a weak and shallow individual whose inane attempts to embroil Angela to become a partner in his non-kosher activities backfired on him as usual. Angela knew that if he refused to behave, he would continually be on the move. Why did he flee to the USA? One theory is that he would try to continue his bad lifestyle and have his details on police records in the UK. There were no folk in the USA to point a finger at him. Of course, that depended on his behaviour.

Chapter Twelve
Life post-divorce

A few years passed. Angela retrained and eventually got herself permanent work. That lasted a few years until a work-related injury, exploitation and a physical attack by an intruder one evening as she slept forced her into early retirement. It resulted in Post-Traumatic Stress Disorder (PTSD) for seven to eight years and she had to retrain herself to concentrate, to read, to comprehend what was read and to recognise familiar people. Suppliers and others who had sent letters and they were not responded to within certain timelines, were left to her daughter to deal with. Soon though, her daughter who had her own young family and work uncertainties became tetchy and distant.

Angela lived in her grandson's room for seven months. The police told her that she needed to feel safe after the intruder attack and living on her own was not an option. Those were empty days for her. Everything around seemed unfamiliar and she could not work through the situation in her mind. Then, an acquaintance told her of a possible secure house which she could apply for. She did so and moved in to live there for the next ten years (until 2010). Her thinking was not fully clear, but she had decided to move on.

An argument with Angela's youngest during this period left her confused. It was over a set of pottery bowls, which her daughter had brought back from Portugal. They were used in Angela's kitchen and when her daughter moved, Angela was unable to understand why her daughter would claim them. No amount of reasoning convinced her to the contrary until years later when she was reminded of that it, with a bit of shared mirth.

After eight or nine years, clarity began to return. She attempted a few activities to keep herself occupied. Her love of languages led her to explore Greek for biblical purposes but her Greek never continued past the request of a bottle of retsina. So, she turned to Hebrew and learned more than enough to read its biblical form. The oral form never developed because of lack of interaction with Hebrew speakers. She had a limited knowledge of German and an eclectic mix of music. Since her concentration was not good, listening to tapes or CDs was a non-starter. Art was a relaxing subject and gardening, where she could watch plants and flowers grow and bloom. By this time, all three of the children had moved away to pursue their own interests.

PTSD is a complete shutdown from reality. Its victims appear to function as normal, but awareness of people and events becomes sort of vague. One is able to be a witness but is unable to empathise or feel part of anything. Not able to read and comprehend and those eight years were a long time. This happened not because of one bad event but because there were too many problems to solve in a short time. The condition rendered its victim to exist with the rest of humanity without feeling part of life.

Angela recalled her response at her GP's diagnosis – 'oh isn't that something which people used to claim compensation?' The doctor replied: 'Maybe, but you have it.' That didn't help as she was unable to comprehend day to day urgencies and needed to apologise continuously for her oversight. She recalled a vague feeling of disembodiment when a woman who had sat next to her on a bus journey into the city, had alighted and Angela seemed to recognise her but was unable to remember where. Months later that picture returned to her memory and she knew who it was. Of course, the woman never spoke on that journey and Angela was totally unaware of someone beside her that day.

Chapter Thirteen
Retirement

It was with great reluctance that she would need to accept that she was no longer needed as a mother, or for work. With a new zeal to explore and learn about the Bible she found stability and comfort and continued in faith to learn to trust in that unseen God for her every need. Why not acknowledge His continuous protection throughout her life? She felt as if she was on her way home, and with renewed vigour aimed to gain as much knowledge as she could: its history, its people, archaeology and anything which might increase knowledge and understanding of those scriptures. It was all so very fascinating and full of intrigue. She wanted to become more informed than simply attending church services, to listen to brief readings and join in joyful singing with others. It was for her a case of "what's it all about? Why bother? Would it help me to understand who I am"?

God the Creator she found to be the least costly and the most thorough and reliable psychotherapist: lots of patience with His subjects; healing continuously where necessary; making His subjects aware of their faults to allow each of them to correct attitude, behaviour and learn to care. It was a slower but a more thorough process which she eventually appreciated. Everything and everyone around seemed to be in a hurry. Going nowhere fast! Her brain appeared to manage at a more slower pace. Dealing with everyday activity was all right until a problem arose and she tried not to panic, to put whatever it was aside and to relax before she dealt with it. Of course, she had had a few counselling sessions during the PTSD period but never could get past the initial relating of her past. No further treatments meant that she was left in limbo to make decisions which in reality she was unable to make.

Folk who are not interested in the acceptance of a Creator often utter silly remarks such as 'oh, she had found God!' That is inaccurate. If there was Divine assistance during her entire lifetime when she was lost how could He be found and where? He was there all the time. No, it was Angela who had finally acknowledged His presence. He had found her even before she was knee high to a grasshopper. He had continued to nurture and protect. Her own father she had barely known up to the age of three, and she was left with her Mum who would struggle to provide for her and her sister. In her entire existence she was aware of how someone, somewhere had been there to rescue her.

Angela had felt that she was in a whirlwind, which spun her out of reality and control. Somehow an unseen Divine hand had supported her and led her away from the eye towards a gentler existence outside. That hurricane was also her healing receptacle, she thought. It would attempt to whirl her back to a place where she would mentally be able to recover its aftereffects and feel energised to move forward. Gradually, confusion waned and mental clarity replaced those lost years. No storm lasts forever and she would clear away the debris to find that new path. She had existed within a vacuum for over forty years, and through prayer had received small snippets as reminders of her past. Emotions, people, everything that was foggy, and grey had been revealed in a new dawn. Human counsel was not sufficiently in-depth enough. It was costly and based on human perspective only.

This was totally thanks to the gentle nurture, encouragement and non-judgemental treatment of church communities including counselling, loads of patience and empathy on her seemingly lengthy road to reality. Knowledge she had yearned for was freely taught and a sense of fun added to that pleasurable trip. Yes, it had been a lot of fun and enjoyment, but also with some questionable interpretations which would take years to learn that not all folk have the ability to be honest or truthful. They were just as eager to know but too ready with answers that left more questions for others. These simple words of hope had kept Angela existing instead of seeking to destroy herself:

When there were two sets of footprints, I had walked with you;

When there was only one set of footprints I had carried you.

She was married to a control freak, a bully, a liar a man who would attempt to kill her rather than divorce her because that would cost him money he was loath to spend on her. He was not to be trusted, a husband in name only, neither a friend nor a companion nor a lover, a fantasist for sure and worst of all an apology for a father. In his desire to destroy Angela he was blind to the reality that he was also destroying his children. He had definitely divided them, and that division continues to the present day. The middle daughter whom he considered his, only daughter declared that Dad could not help it. It was not his fault that things went wrong. She remains under that delusion.

No, he deserved no sympathy. He had made a conscious decision to live selfishly to satisfy his own desires. In emigrating to the USA, he had chosen to run and hide but he could not run forever and would always need a base. He had probably surmised that no one in the USA would reproach him or be aware of his deceptions. It was a place of safety for him, no consequences to bother him, not even his own children. Then there was the son he had boasted of leaving behind in Germany and with Angela for a shield, the child in Ireland. Angela had no doubt that he had eventually used her in his urgency for a new life. He would not agree to Angela divorcing him though. It was too much for his weak ego - as his reason to leave the UK would be that HE had divorced his wife for whatever reason. That would be more to his agreement – to be in control.

Does Angela have any regrets about this whole episode? No. Just one. When she became desperate for Francis to leave and he wouldn't, she thought of a way she had hoped that would encourage him to leave. She wrote an insulting letter to his eldest sister. Its purpose was to enrage her to cause her to contact her brother and to advise him to leave Angela. It mattered not what she would have said, as long he left. Angela had no way of knowing if this warped strategy worked but it was a relief when he did leave. She deeply regretted this because that person had been kind to her. She had never, to Angela's knowledge, said any unkind words, but Angela was forced to resort to desperate means to rid herself of that weak bully she saw affecting not only herself but her children.

Angela recently wondered what would Francis have become if she had not become his nemesis? How recurring were her experiences throughout the years? The parallels with her mother's demise? How, ironic it was that she ran away from her influential family's interference, to be independent yet she had a husband who wanted to aspire to be respectable but was too weak a character to ever reach that goal?

Angela meanwhile spent years recovering from the hatred, the ultimate loathing of that "fourth child" who served as her controller. She was ostracised and humiliated to the point of despair. However, that Divine Provider held on to her to bring her gradually through the storms which raged inside and around her. She emerged and became aware that she was slowly being divested of her dignity, her self-esteem. She was never in that race for wealth or renown just opportunities to provide comfort for herself in later life. Ultimately, she acknowledged that the girls would leave to forge their own paths in life and she was reluctant to depend on them or on anyone else to provide her with the necessities for life, but even that was stripped from her. She had found peace through patience which she needed to learn. There is no more hatred just the occasional bouts of irritability at the practices and self-serving attitude of many around. They received adequate opportunities for advancement with free sound education, then wasted these on bullying others to provide them with 'their rights to'. Except that what is considered as a right is merely a privilege. Nor is happiness a human right. Contentment and stability are truer goals to aim for.

It had been a long harrowing journey to peace and someone once remarked to Angela that she had paid a high price for freedom. True, but she could have gladly foregone the trials. On the other hand, she has learned a tome of lessons, for retirement! If her faculties remain intact, that is! Today, Angela has been able to sing these few lines. Someone said that it's from an old hymn or song:

I sing because I am happy,
I sing because I am free,
His eyes are on the sparrow.
And I know He watches me.

Angela: "A bird with a broken wing".

The Moravian Church in Queenstown

The Victoria Amazonia White Lily.

Its flower is pure White and it is the national flower of Guyana. This is the largest lily and its leaves can grow to three metres in diameter. Its stalk may reach up to eight metres.

A Sloth.
Exclusive tree dwellers within the forest

A Coconut Grove.

The coconuts are hacked off from bunches above, then collected and transported for processing. Some old or ripened ones are cut open, husked and again hacked opened from its nut to reveal hard white flesh. Un-ripened coconuts are also collected for market and street stall vendors to sell as a nourishing refreshing drink in the warm climate.

A wide variety of Vegetables

. The Kaiteur Falls
A world wonder a single drop of 228metres.

Family
Judges & Jurors at a family function

Wedding
After the ceremony 1966

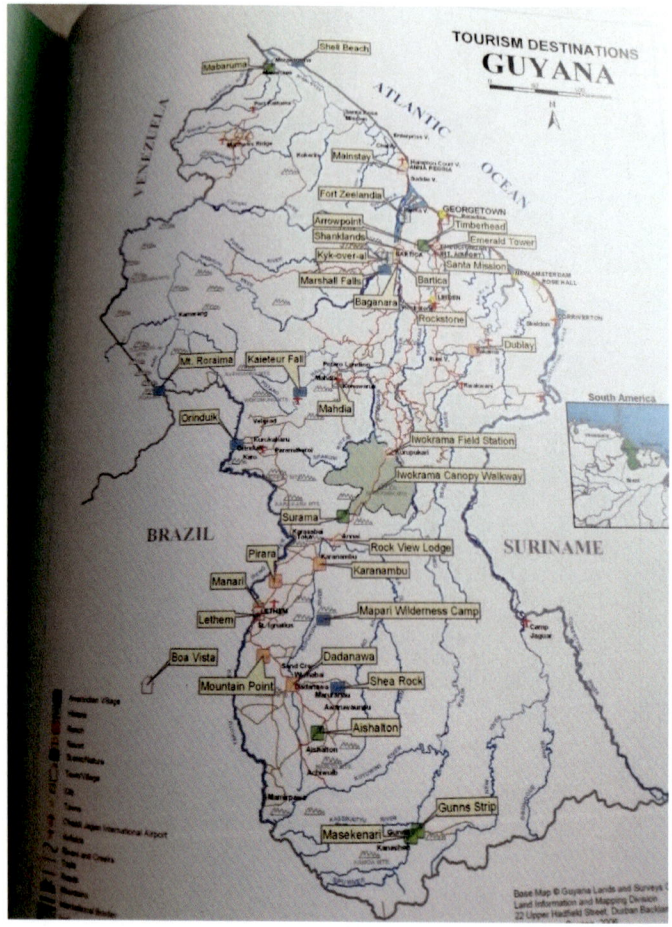

A Map of Guyana

The land of many waters, falls including the famous Kaieteur Falls with its straight drop, rivers, streams and trenches.